Baby Teacher

Nurturing Neural Networks from Birth to Age Five

Rebecca Shore

A SCARECROWEDUCATION BOOK

The Scarecrow Press, Inc.
Lanham, Maryland, and London
2002

A SCARECROWEDUCATION BOOK

Published in the United States of America
by Scarecrow Press, Inc.
4720 Boston Way, Lanham, Maryland 20706
www.scarecrowpress.com

4 Pleydell Gardens, Folkestone
Kent CT20 2DN, England

British Library Cataloguing in Publication Information Available

Library of Congress Cataloging-in-Publication Data

Shore, Rebecca, 1957-
    Baby teacher : nurturing neural networks from birth to age five /
Rebecca Shore.
        p. cm.
    Includes bibliographical references (p.   ).
    ISBN 0-8108-4284-X (pbk. : alk. paper)
    1. Child development.   2. Infants—Development.   3. Early childhood
education.   I. Title.

LB1115 .S63 2002
155.42'3—dc21

                                2002001888

This book is dedicated to my first teachers,
Bruce and Wynona, my parents; and

my most profound teachers,
Leigh and Bobby, my children;

and my husband, Marcus,
who continually shows me alternative ways of learning.

With deepest gratitude to *all* of the
wonderful teachers in the world,
especially the carpenter's son and
the Old Wig

Contents

List of Figures   vii

Acknowledgments   ix

Introduction   xi

1   Finding Faulty Assumptions   1

2   Brain Science for Nonneurologists   11

3   How We Know What We Know   25

4   Nurturing Our Nature   45

5   Music Matters   57

6   The Bach Effect   81

7   Implications for Education   113

8   Curricular Considerations   143

9   Creating Complex Curriculum
for the Crib and Beyond   153

Bibliography   179

About the Author   185

Figures

Yosemite National Park, Ansel Adams   xv

Portrait of a Neuron   13

Neural Networks   16

The Basic Brain   17

The Triune Brain   22

Music Era Time Line   65

Wolfgang Amadeus Mozart   66

Johann Sebastian Bach   87

Comparison of Three Musical Textures   90

Acknowledgments

My sincere thanks to those dear friends who read early versions of the manuscripts and gave me their invaluable feedback: Bonnie Bruce, Dr. Fenwick English, Dr. Beverly Jones III, Dr. Gordon Shaw, Dr. Daniel Sher, Dr. Bruce Brasher and his wonderful wife, Cindy, Bruce and Wynona Martin, Melissa Dowd, Joel Whitten, and Ellen Wenner. Your suggestions helped clarify and focus my voice.

Special thanks to Kathryn Bornac and Melissa Dowd for their creative illustrations and their assistance with dreaded technological and computer-assisted design aspects of the book and to Bobbie Collins at Wake Forest University for her research assistance. Thanks go to Dr. Lorraine Cooke, of the New Jersey Association for the Education of Young Children, for her contribution to the New Jersey story. Also, special thanks to the Mom's Night Out group, and especially Janet, for their support of a mom writer in progress.

A tremendous debt of gratitude to Lawrence Paulson, my incredible copyeditor, and Cheryl Hoffman, of Hoffman-Paulson Associates; and to Shirley, Cindy, Amos, Mary Jo, and the wonderful team at Scarecrow Press.

And finally, thank you to my children, Leigh and Bobby, from the bottom of Mommy's heart, for igniting the initial spark of inspiration for this literary child, *Baby Teacher*.

Introduction:
Eye-Opening Discoveries

Thinking can never be unseasonable.
—Wolfgang Amadeus Mozart,
in a letter to his father December 15, 1781

Have you ever traveled in a country that doesn't speak your language? Perhaps you found yourself in a shop needing an answer to an important question. You ask a salesperson, "Where is the rest room?" The salesperson looks at you, but you soon discover that she does not understand a word of what you asked. Do you then repeat your question more slowly and perhaps more loudly? "W h e r e i s y o u r r e s t r o o m ?" Perhaps you speak English and your potential information source speaks only Japanese or Farsi. Perhaps the salesperson's language doesn't even use the same alphabet as yours.

If this particular scenario has never happened to you, you have probably seen it happen to others or portrayed in movies, plays, or television programs. Step back from it now and analyze some obviously faulty assumptions that you intuitively relied upon. Does the salesperson have a hearing impairment? You have no data to support this assumption. She did look at you when you spoke. Yet you automatically raised your voice in an attempt to communicate better. Did the salesperson misunderstand your pronunciation? Perhaps. However, you could speak at a speed that would make a southerner sound like a New Yorker and it would never be slow enough for your potential information source to understand if her language is different. This effort to communicate by speaking louder and slower was based on faulty assumptions.

Don't feel too bad. There was a time when the planet Earth was believed to be flat and left-handedness was considered a human defect, and even a time when non-Euro-Americans were not considered to be human. Fortunately, as more and more seemingly correct assumptions have been disproved, we have become a society more inclined to consider alternative views. Fortunately, we have evolved as a people.

This book is about potentially faulty assumptions—assumptions that can actually stifle the development of your most prized contribution to life, your baby or young child. If you are a parent, teacher, or caregiver, you could at best be missing magical moments in the child's life that can never be returned to and at worst could be harming his or her development.

This book proposes that infants and young children can take in and process far more complex data from their environment than was previously thought. In fact, the complex data and enriched environment actually increase neural networking in the infant brain. The wonderful world we live in doesn't have to be watered down for babies but simply presented to them in a conscientious manner, one that works for them developmentally. Contrary to popular belief today, It is my contention that babies come to us hardwired for receiving complex data. Only through receiving this stimulation will they maximize their God-given potential brainpower.

This book is inspired by a true story: the story of what happened to me when research coincided with real life. And as is so often the case, real life became the greater of the learning experiences. Research only tries to describe and give order to it. Ask Jean Piaget. Ask John Dewey.

In the Beginning

In 1994, I got a big surprise. I found out that I was pregnant. I was thirty-seven years old and had never slowed down long enough even to think about the possibility of bearing children. I had just defended my doctoral dissertation and was ready to finish my research study and write it all up. I was working full-time as an assistant principal at a large comprehensive high school in southern California, teaching at a local university, and trying to find ways to fix our country's education system. As fate would have it, becoming a mother was going to be added to my résumé of life's experiences. It was also to become the most wonderful experience in my life—greater than any job I ever held, any degrees I ever earned, anything I ever accomplished. And perhaps most important, it would become my greatest *learning* experience, leading me to what I am now confident is the answer to our education system's problems.

When I found out that I was pregnant, I began voraciously devouring everything in print about early childhood. After almost two decades of working in secondary schools, I knew a lot about adolescents but very little about babies. Fortunately, my quest to fix schools had already led to an interest in the brain and how and why learning occurs the way it does.

Seeing Is Believing

In becoming a self-made early childhood expert in the mid-1990s, I had read all of the latest research about infant development. Of particular interest to me was the research on sight. I found this interesting because it showed me how little we had looked through the eyes of babies throughout history and how we had designed baby environments around what we saw instead of what they saw.

I read the research reporting that babies were not born with the ability to distinguish pinks and blues and all of those other light pastel colors that parents had traditionally used to decorate babies' cribs and bedrooms. That sophistication would develop a little later. The research said that the vision of babies operated best when viewing sharp contrasts, namely, objects in black and white.[1] Always looking for opportunities to apply research, I was one of those progressive moms who bought a black-and-white crib mobile when they first hit the market, instead of one of the pretty pink ones.

I read several new books that recommended using black-and-white flash cards with babies to stimulate their visual neural networks. I had also seen the baby flash cards when they first arrived in stores: white cards with a black circle, triangles, parallel lines, and so forth. While I'm no artist, I was confident that I could re-create those simple flash cards for less than $7.95! So yes, I admit it. I went to the local office supply store and bought white cardboard and black markers and made my own.

My daughter, Leigh, loved working with flash cards. She would smile and giggle and obviously enjoyed the activity. However, she rarely looked at the cards. She was always looking at (laughing at) Mommy. (She did, however, love to chew on the cards and bend them into interesting shapes.)

When Leigh was about five months old, I noticed something that initiated much thinking and questioning and ultimately led to the writing of this book. I was holding Leigh while looking through a stack of mail on the counter. She was clearly mesmerized by a particular picture hanging on our kitchen wall. It was a large black-and-white print of an Ansel Adams photograph of Yosemite National Park.

What surprised me about Leigh's attention to this particular photo was not just the intensity of her long gaze but also the incredible complexity of what she was looking at. Her body language, that evidence that all baby researchers rely upon so heavily, made clear to me that she was taking in much data from this activity. She was also enjoying it and did not want to stop. I was quickly reminded of one of my favorite quotes by Renate Caine, who at a conference of school administrators had explained that research showed that "the mind is virtually inexhaustible when it is engaged in something it perceives as meaningful."[2] The lower portion of the picture, the area at which Leigh was directly staring, depicted hundreds of pine trees covered with light snow. There were patterns, yes, but not simple, regular, man-made patterns. Each tree had a trunk with protruding branches. The number of lines created by all of those tree branches must have reached into

© Ansel Adams Publishing Rights Trust/CORBIS

the hundreds of thousands, and just like the mind of every child, every tree was slightly different—a far cry from the simple lines and shapes on the flash cards sold in the baby stores.

Babies may not be able to see light colors, but it seemed to me that in the colors they could see—blacks, whites, and other sharply contrasting hues—they were able to distinguish highly complex images. Different did not necessarily mean *simpler*. It just meant different. It occurred to me that perhaps my husband and I should just drive up to Yosemite and show Leigh the reality of its magnificence in person. But research abounds that infant vision doesn't extend much beyond a foot—just about the distance from mom's breast to her face. Obviously distance vision isn't necessary in the womb, so vision in a newborn is not yet well developed at birth. In fact, a newborn baby's eyesight is roughly 20/500.[3] Early researchers assumed that babies were not interested in objects more than a foot or so away from them. This, I would argue, was a faulty assumption. The truth is, they just couldn't see them clearly!

Some promoters of the simple flash cards claim that the overly simple black-and-white pictures for babies help them learn to focus more quickly. However, more recent research suggests that the cards can only help babies focus in the first ten to twelve days of life, if then. By week three, babies are focusing just fine on those simple black-and-white symbols and are ready for more. More what? More complexity.

I had also read the research that claimed that babies seem to like looking at human faces. And whose face do they seem to like best? Mom's, of course. Again I saw the flash cards arrive in the baby stores. Again I took one look at those simple smiley faces drawn on card stock and re-created them myself. And again Leigh clearly preferred my face to the drawings on the cards.

What is it about a human face that seems to so engage babies? Early researchers suggested that it may help babies distinguish different people. However, a baby's sense of smell is highly sensitive at birth and would surely help to accomplish that task easily in infancy. On the other hand, ask any anatomy professor which area of the human body is the most complex to view and he will say the human face. The face has many muscles and movable parts and it is obviously expressive beyond quantification. The data transmitted by the combination of the facial muscles, eyes, lips, teeth, tongue, eyebrows, forehead, and even nostrils are exponentially more complex than those conveyed by any other part of the body. The subtle and quick changes from expression to expression add a depth to the complexity of the vision that photographs or flash cards cannot capture. At last count, the face transmits over seven thousand expressions.[4] Furthermore, have you ever seen a more expressive face than that of a mother gazing at her newborn? No pleasure is more joyful and no concern more fearful. The human face is a tremendously complex data transmitter, and babies love it. Mom's face is even more dynamic, and babies love it even more.

A week or two after the picture incident with Leigh, I heard the remark, "You have to crawl before you walk and walk before you run." The underlying assumption, so common in our culture, was that we have to move from the simple to the more complex. It's a concept that is certainly deeply embedded in our education system.

In some cases, it may even be true. But after interviewing several prominent doctors, I found that in terms of the brain and body working together, moving from a sedentary position to mobility—crawling—is a much more complex task for a baby than moving from walking to running is for a child. The point is that perhaps we have underestimated the functioning of the infant mind. And perhaps the simple truth is that developmentally appropriate complexity builds better-functioning brains.

Just where is the line between abuse or neglect and enrichment? Is feeding, clothing, and not shaking our babies really enough? Are we only interested in the *survival* of our youngest citizens? Or do we truly care about the whole child? Cognitive development in very young children has been misunderstood for centuries and overshadowed by attention to their physical, social, and emotional growth and development. Unfortunately, those aspects of a child's development are intricately linked to the child's brain. What about a child's future ability to participate fully in a democratic society or to learn language and read and think? The study of newborns appears to be a classic case of what is now called the "positivist fallacy."[5] This is a fallacy that arises when we infer that absence of evidence *is* evidence of absence. When it comes to the cognitive development of babies, this faulty assumption has certainly clouded our view.

Consider how a newborn baby acquires language. What evidence can babies show behavioral psychologists that would suggest they are learning language? Psychologists measure and record such behaviors as breathing, heartbeat, and sucking and try to conclude whether a baby shows more or less interest in a particular activity. Unfortunately, none of these behaviors appears to provide the evidence needed to determine what complex mental representations are forming in their little brains. Should we wait to speak to a child until the child can speak? Of course we shouldn't, even though it is largely through anecdotal evidence that we conclude that infants learn language long before they can give us evidence of that learning. It is through hearing language and being spoken to that babies learn language themselves, long before the first "mama" emerges.

Newborn babies know much, much more than we have ever previously realized. More important, however, is how much they could know. What is the potential learning capacity of a newborn? Unfortunately, babies don't initially appear to know much of anything, or if they do, they can't readily communicate it to us. Therefore historically, on the great continuum of knowing, babies have been viewed as existing on the opposite end from the great philosophers.[6]

Babies arrive in this world helpless. Their physical development, their very survival depends almost entirely upon the behaviors of the caregivers in their environment. So traditionally, it has been the health and safety of babies that has concerned parents and other care providers. But what about the cognitive development of children? When do they become educable? When do they learn to think? They may not upon first blush appear to be thinking machines at all. We know now, however, that they are in fact incredibly high-powered thinking machines. They have more brain cells at birth than at any other time in their lives. Later, the brain cells prune themselves—"use them or lose them," as the saying goes. Babies who have been neglected physically show outward signs of the neglect rather early. Battering leaves bruises. Insufficient nutrition can often be detected through the size of the baby or other physical cues. The effects of cognitive neglect, however, may not show up until the child reaches kindergarten—which, tragically, may be too late to overcome them. Deprived of stimulation, connections in the brain that could become neural networks of high-level thinking and understanding do not connect later on. Babies simply have not been able to communicate this to us in a language that we can easily understand. Fortunately, modern technology is helping us to decode their understanding at breathtaking speed. The critical implications of this new outpouring of data need rapid dissemination.

Failure to nurture complex neural networks and thus lay a strong, broad foundation in the infant brain upon which higher-level thought may later be formed has significantly more tragic consequences than our prior historical misunderstandings because the neglect of the infant brain cannot be overcome or corrected later in life, except in the most unusual of circumstances. The cumulative unfulfilled potential that has resulted from this neglect is mind-boggling.

At this point, the past possibilities of greatly increased brain-power are spilled milk. We cannot go backward. However, with the incredible advances in brain research brought about by modern technology, we no longer have excuses for any sparrows arriving at the kindergarten door; all children can and should be bluebirds by age five. This is not a book about creating "superbabies." It is a book that is dedicated to helping every single child develop his full, innate potential.

Notes

1. Penelope Leach, *Your Baby and Child: From Birth through Age Five,* rev. ed. (New York: Alfred A. Knopf, 2000), 13.

2. Renate Nummela Caine and Geoffrey Caine, "Understanding a Brain-Based Approach to Learning and Teaching," *Educational Leadership* 48, no. 2 (October 1990): 66–70.

3. Thomas Verny with John Kelly, The Secret Life of the Unborn Child (New York: Dell, 1981), 40.

4. John Cleese, "The Human Face," *Newsweek,* August 27, 2001, 5.

5. David Huron, "Music and Mind: Foundations of Cognitive Musicology" (lecture 1 of the 1999 Ernest Bloch Lecture Series at the University of California at Berkeley, September–December 1999). Available at dactyl.som.ohio-state.edu/Music220/Bloch.lectures/Bloch.lectures.html.

6. Alison Gopnik, Andrew N. Meltzoff, and Patricia K. Kuhl, *The Scientist in the Crib* (New York: Morrow, 1999), 12..

Finding Faulty Assumptions

Error flies from mouth to mouth, from pen to pen,
and to destroy it takes ages.

—Voltaire

"What if the world really isn't flat?" Early astronomers con-
templated this notion, although they usually did it quietly because
of the political and religious ramifications if it were found to be
true. In 1492, Christopher Columbus helped prove those early
astronomers correct: the earth wasn't flat after all! Then in 1530,
Nicolas Copernicus released his great work, *De Revolutionibus,* in
which he suggested that the earth rotated around the sun and not
vice versa. This new knowledge could not initially penetrate the
belief that the earth was the center of God's universe. Two great
Italian scientists, Bruno and Galileo, believed Copernicus. Bruno
was burned at the stake. In 1633, Galileo was tortured into
renouncing this belief. His life was spared, although he spent the
rest of his days in prison.[1] Truth can have tragic consequences.

"All men are created equal" were the now infamous words of
the great American Thomas Jefferson. All men, that is, except for
Indians, Africans, Aborigines, Jews, women—the list could go on
and on. Manifest Destiny, slavery, and the Holocaust represent just

a few of the more tragic by-products of our misconceptions. In this case, the misconception was of the definition of the word "men."

Throughout history, our realization of greater truths, our cumulative societal evolution as a species on this planet, has often resulted from recognition that our prior thinking was based on faulty assumptions, assumptions that may have once appeared true or real to us but became obviously erroneous—often embarrassingly so and often with tragic consequences.

A recent—though less-than-tragic—case is that of left-handedness. There was a time when left-handedness was considered to be the result of a defect of some kind. (Lefties probably would not consider this less than tragic!) Children in school who exhibited left-handed tendencies were forced to learn to write with their right hands. This view of left-handedness resulted in some less-than-flattering expressions in our language, such as "left-handed compliment." The words "sinister" and "gauche" are derived from the Latin and French words for "left."

The earth was initially considered flat because that's the way it appeared to the unaided human eye. Since a straight horizon was all man could see at the time, how could the earth possibly be round? And if it looked flat to them at the time, with their limited vision capabilities (including their limited vision of what could come along in the future to enhance and expand our "vision"), the assumption was made that the world was, in fact, flat. Initially, Indians, Africans, Aborigines, and others were considered nonhuman by Europeans because these people could not communicate with the dominant society. Their language was unintelligible and they shared a different culture from the dominant culture of their geographic location at the time. Consequently, they were not believed to be human or to have souls and, therefore, mistreating or killing them was considered no more immoral than mistreating or killing any other beast. Two hundred years ago, women in the United States were not permitted to vote, own their own homes, or sign contracts. They used the events surrounding the Emancipation Proclamation to gain rights for their gender. Today we continue to strive for universal recognition of, and respect for, all people, regardless of their language, culture, age, gender, or other differences.

Lefties were considered faulty because they wrote, threw, and used knives and forks differently from the majority. Thanks to modern technological developments in brain research, we now know that the corpus callosum, the brain part that helps the left and right hemispheres communicate, is actually 11 percent larger in lefties. And while lefties make up only about 10 percent of the population, left-handedness is much more common among mathematicians, musicians, architects, artists, and professional baseball players—not a motley crew to be among! Who would object to possessing the talents of a Leonardo da Vinci, Michelangelo, Albert Einstein, Benjamin Franklin, or Sandy Kofax, left-handed or not?

In each of these examples, the truth was "different," yes, but "faulty," no.

The commonality among these scenarios is that they come from the ugly list of the unfortunate results of thinking and acting upon faulty assumptions. Throughout history these faulty assumptions have resulted in the loss or ruin of countless lives, leaving an embarrassing blemish on our evolutionary history.

The subject of this book is another tragedy based on a faulty assumption. It is a tragedy whose pain is easily overlooked but that exceeds any other in history because it has been and continues to be so pervasive and far-reaching. There is no way to calculate its cumulative loss over the generations of civilized humanity. The misunderstanding addressed here is that of the infant brain and its remarkable capabilities when properly nurtured in the first years of life. Genetics matter. But intelligence is not fixed at birth. Environment matters so very much that it can, by conservative estimates, alter IQ by twenty to forty points in either direction, depending upon the environmental circumstances of a newborn baby.[2] The environment of the first few years of life can truly make or break our intellectual futures. We are our brains. And since so much of what is considered "success" in life rides upon the facility of the brain, failure to do everything possible to maximize the potential of every child not only falls short of preserving the common good, it also creates the common bad. It is only through increased complexity in the data received by the brain in early childhood that more complex neural networks can form, creating a foundation for increased brain capacity in later life. Nurturing neural networks is as important as providing food for tummies and clean diapers on bottoms.

Complexity Defined

Webster's Seventh New Collegiate Dictionary says something that is complex is "a whole made up of complicated or interrelated parts; a group of obviously related units of which the degree and nature of the relationship is imperfectly known; hard to separate, analyze, or solve; a . . . substance in which the constituents are more intimately associated than in a simple mixture." A usage note says, "Complex suggests the unavoidable result of a necessary combining or folding and does not imply a fault or failure; complicated applies to what offers great difficulty in understanding, solving, or explaining." Some of Webster's definitions of the term "simple" include "not complex," "innocent," "uneducated," "easy, straightforward, causing little difficulty." Which of these words or phrases have you heard most frequently with reference to babies?

There is abundant research indicating that parents who speak more words to their infants will usually hear their children speak words back sooner and in more abundance. Parents who use more complex sentence structures when talking to their babies, using phrases that include words such as "which" and "because," generally hear seven- and eight-word sentences back from their children long before parents with simpler speech habits. While babies cannot talk to us in their infancy, they clearly absorb and work with as much data as they are exposed to; the more complex the data input, the more complex and sophisticated the output. This is documented in Betty Hart and Todd Risley's 1995 book, *Meaningful Differences in the Everyday Experiences of Young American Children,* which describes their longitudinal study of the effects of the behavior of parents on the cognitive development of their offspring. The amount of data they gathered over the years that the study encompassed would fill fifteen books (twenty-three megabytes of computer storage area). To summarize their findings in a few sentences: They found that the more educated the mother, the more she spoke to her child. Less-educated moms of low socioeconomic status spoke the least. By the age of three, children of educated, professional parents had heard approximately thirty million words. Children of working-class parents had heard about twenty million, and children of moms with low socioeconomic standing around ten million. As might be expected, the vocabularies and IQs of the professional parents dwarfed those of the welfare parents.

There was also a difference in the quality of the words spoken to the children. Professional parents were quick and generous with positive feedback to their children, while welfare parents were much more critical. The development of the three-year-olds was followed and studied until the children reached the third grade. The early parental behaviors continued, and researchers predicted correctly that performance on language and IQ tests continued to be higher for the children of professional parents.

So clear is the research on speaking to babies that it can be expected that unless brain abnormalities of some kind are present, a child's speaking ability will be a direct result of the stimulation that he receives early in life, not genetic or socioeconomic factors. In contrast, a child who is not exposed to complex speech patterns early in life usually never develops them. In Noam Chomsky's 1988 book, *Language and Problems of Knowledge*, he writes, "It is something that happens to the child placed in an appropriate environment." There appear to be no limits on the level of complexity of speech that the infant brain can process given an enriched, complex environment. Research shows that it is far simpler to learn second and third languages as a young child than as a teenager. This fact alone has implications with respect to complexity and the infant brain. More recent research shows us that a newborn baby comes into the world able to distinguish all of the possible human sounds produced by every language in the world. Yet after only a year of life, babies no longer have the capacity to hear such subtleties and complexity. They can only hear those sounds they have repeatedly heard during their first year of life. This is almost always the language spoken in their home environment.[3]

Clearly, complexity is a critical concept with regard to the acquisition of speech. When neurons in babies' brains experience multiple languages or more-complex speech patterns in their environment, they do what they were born to do—connect. They create a neural network that is itself more complex than a neural network created by exposure to less-complex stimuli.

The Nature (or Nurture) of Intelligence

The specific faulty assumption that managed to blind researchers of the first half of the twentieth century, and continues to prevail in the thinking of many educators and parents today, is this: Intelligence is fixed. It is determined genetically at birth and remains the same until death. The roots of this misconception lie in a simple oversight. In the mid-1800s, when Charles Darwin was investigating the origin of the species, his cousin, Francis Galton, became curious about the heritability of human intelligence. Galton's study of the differences between individual human beings overlooked the influence of environmental factors. This oversight probably caused the persistence of the concept of fixed intelligence. Many intelligence tests, even many used today, were developed according to this faulty assumption.

The social consequences of this assumption are clear. In eighteenth-century Europe, babies were born and grew into children basically on their own. At some point, their intelligence was assessed, and they took their place in what was considered to be the natural hierarchy of society: the haves, the have-nots, and a few in between. The American dream of all people being created equal was not yet a twinkle in the founding fathers' eyes. And when the U.S. Constitution was written, the concept of all people being created equal was one that, in practice, did not actually include all people. Who could have imagined the lives that would be lost and the processes that would have to be undertaken to achieve a society that today more closely resembles the concept of equality?

In 1905, the French government commissioned Alfred Binet to develop a test that would separate the slow learners from the "more intelligent" in schools. The prevailing assumption was that slow learners could not become more intelligent and therefore should not be allowed to hold the faster learners back. They should be sorted out. Binet's writings of the time reveal that he did not believe that intelligence was fixed; he suggested that it was "educable." Yet somehow this aspect of his views and research was not taken seriously for six decades. The Stanford-Binet Intelligence Scale test was a combined effort of Binet and Lewis Terman of Stanford University. The original test, created in 1921, was used to sort students in schools for curricular programs, to sort people in the military for rank or placement, and to help determine future vocations. Despite Binet's view, the way IQ (intelligence quotient) numbers were used reflected a belief that intelligence is fixed. Surprisingly, even today revised versions of the test reflect a fixed-intelligence assumption.

Throughout the 1930s and 1940s, testing became particularly popular in and outside school. In addition to scholastic aptitude testing, tests were used for everything from assisting with career planning to choosing the best personality in a future wife or husband. In schools, the IQ of children was kept secret from parents. Educators believed that since this magic number, determined usually around age six, predicted mental capacity, it could not be entrusted to the general public. (Some schools today are still hesitant to share this information with parents.)

A logical outgrowth of this notion of fixed intelligence was that of predeterminism. If children were programmed from birth to develop in a particular way regardless of environmental factors, why should their growth be guided at all? Some educators recommended that parents simply watch their children "bloom like a flower" and not interfere. In light of present research revealing the importance of the adult role in the environment, this permissivism borders on child abuse.

Fortunately, over time, some dissonant data began to appear. Evidence began to emerge that suggested that IQ is not fixed. The earlier work of Maria Montessori, who developed a system of early childhood care, is an example and is discussed further in chapter 3. She, like Binet, believed that a person's intelligence was educable, and she set out to prove it. And while her work was tremendously successful, it was extremely slow to be recognized and accepted. It took many more years of similar research to begin to turn the tide. Many educators and psychologists in the 1940s and 1950s risked their reputations by producing evidence that intelligence may not be fixed. Among them were many female professors, who also may have faced credibility questions because of their gender.

Finally, in the 1960s, studies on orphan children in model nursery schools became too dramatic to ignore. Following up on the work begun by Beth Wellman at Iowa University in 1938, Harold M. Skeels and Harold B. Dye found that children removed from the original orphanage and placed in a significantly more stimulating environment gained more than twenty IQ points when retested. Even more remarkable, those children left in the orphanage had lost thirteen to forty-five IQ points when retested.[4] Follow-up studies published in 1957 by Wayne Dennis and Pergrouhi Najarian of orphans in Beirut, Lebanon, found that even the maturation and developmental stages of the children could be altered by environment. These researchers presented evidence to support their theory in year-old babies who could not sit up and four-year-olds who could not yet walk. This was so developmentally contrary to every other normal child studied, the only plausible answer was nurture over nature. If intelligence were fixed, these children would have automatically figured out these basic developmental activities regardless of their environment. However, robbed of an appropriate environment for learning even these essential skills, the children reported on in this study had foundered.[5]

Other theories came to light. For example, the work of the Russian researcher Lev Vygotsky, which was long suppressed, eventually was translated into English. Vygotsky believed that learning actually leads development and that intelligence, as well as development, changes constantly as a result. (Vygotsky's work will be further explored in chapter 5.) Combining all of the data from Europe and the United States, a new theory was considered. Perhaps IQ changes. Perhaps the brain can be altered by experience. Perhaps the earth isn't flat.

By the year 1970, the concept of fixed intelligence was considered disproved. More longitudinal studies that followed children from birth into adulthood, with data gathered all along the way, revealed unquestionable changes in IQ scores. In 1964, Jerome Bruner made a profound observation: "The significance about the growth of the mind in the child is not to what degree it depends upon capacity but upon the unlocking of capacity."[6] This process, he reported, could only be accomplished through interaction with the child's environment.

In the 1980s, researchers such as Stephen J. Buell, Paul D. Coleman, and Marian Diamond followed up with studies that proved that if we didn't use our brains, we would actually lose brain capacity. Diamond further reported that remaining curious and active and maintaining a love of life were all-important ingredients for neural tissue in the brain to remain stimulated and healthy. Love of life, self, and others was basic, she said.[7]

Today, we see tremendous gaps between high-achieving kindergartners and children who struggle to identify colors and shapes. Educators report—and research backs up the claim—that if children are experiencing failure in their schoolwork by the end of the third grade, they rarely catch up with their more successful peers. Over time, this lack of success in school can translate into a lack of interest in continuing one's education or, more seriously, discourage learning altogether. The majority of these failing students come from low socioeconomic and minority backgrounds.

Huge sums of federal and foundation funds have been injected into the education system over the last two decades in an attempt to bridge the learning gap. Unfortunately, research abounds indicating that we have not been able to bridge that gap. From the Annenberg millions to the Title I billions, from whole school restructuring efforts to reducing class sizes, from the two decades of Effective Schools research to the Blue Ribbon Schools Conditions for Effective Schools, no silver bullet has surfaced. How can so much hard work, so much money, and the best of intentions fail to produce some kind of "best practices" that work for educating all of our children? Perhaps the critical question is not "How do children learn best?" but "When do children learn best?" Do we believe that children of poverty or children from particular races are genetically incapable of developing performance levels equal to those of their higher-socioeconomic peers? To believe this would be racist and based on a faulty assumption. Clearly, babies learn, and teaching them appropriately changes their brains and their lives.

The development of our brain is critical to the development of our intelligence and our personality. It is a major factor in determining our future options and ultimate life experiences. To fully understand how to develop our brain capacity and that of our babies, we must first understand at least some of the complex structures and functions of our brains.

Notes

1. "The Scientists: Nicolas Copernicus," Blupete.com 1998, www.blupete.com/Literature/Biographies/Copernicus.htm [accessed October 30, 2000].

2. Barbara Clark, *Growing Up Gifted* (Columbus, Ohio: Merrill, 1988), 11.

3. Joan Raymond, "The World of the Senses," *Newsweek,* Fall/Winter 2000 (special issue), 18.

4. Harold M. Skeels and H. B. Dye, "A Study of the Effects of Different Stimulation on Mentally Retarded Children," *Proceedings of the American Association on Mental Deficiency* 44 (1939): 114–36.

5. Wayne Dennis and Pergrouhi Najarian, "Infant Development under Environmental Handicap," *Psychological Monographs* 71, no. 7 (1957): 1–13.

6. Jerome Bruner, "The Course of Cognitive Growth," *American Psychologist* 19 (1964): 1–15.

7. Marian Diamond, "Brain Research and Its Implications for Education" (paper presented at the Twenty-fifth Annual Conference of the California Association for the Gifted, Los Angeles, February 1986).

2

Brain Science
for Nonneurologists

*With our new knowledge of the brain, we are just
dimly beginning to realize that we can now understand humans, including ourselves, as never before,
and that this is the greatest advance of the century,
and quite possibly the most significant in all human
history.*

—*Leslie A. Hart,*
Human Brain and Human Learning

"The Decade of the Brain." This was the title given to the 1990s
by the U.S. Congress because of the explosion of research on the
brain. The pace at which we are now discovering the interplay
between biology, behavior, and the brain is nothing short of exhila-
rating. Almost every day, a new study enlightens us about new
breakthroughs in science, medicine, psychology, and education. We
know now that virtually everything psychological is also biological
and that the brain plays the leading role in the functioning of how
it all plays out.

Welcome to the Century of the Mind. Teachers, psychologists,
pediatricians, and neurologists are uniting in the search for exactly how the brain learns and operates and how better to facilitate

these processes. The brain brings it all together in the body, and it is bringing us all together in the disciplines of knowledge as well. To better understand learning, we must understand a bit about brain functioning. To do this, we must begin with a quick course in Brain Science (for nonneurologists).

Today, we know that the body is made up of cells. These cells "talk" to each other, and the brain is the keeper of the keys to most all of the action. Most cells in the body have specific jobs that they are designed to accomplish. Hair follicle cells grow hair. Muscle cells build tissue with the ability to contract, relax, and grow muscles. Brain cells are born to communicate. They do this through a complex system of electrical and chemical signals from cell to cell. The primary function of the brain is to receive information from all parts of the body, interpret it, and then decide on responses to it.

The adult human brain weighs about three pounds and is roughly the size of a large grapefruit or cantaloupe. It is a fragile mass that is found at the top of the spinal column. It is surrounded by membranes that serve to protect it and is enclosed in the skull for even greater protection. The brain of an adult resembles the texture of Jell-O, while the brain of an infant more closely resembles custard. As any Jell-O and custard connoisseur knows, jarring custard can be much more shape-altering than giving a good jolt to Jell-O that is set. Both substances will wiggle and jiggle, but only custard will change beyond recognition. This is one reason we should never shake a baby. Permanent brain damage and even death may be the result.

Brain Cells

Brain cells were first observed under a microscope in the 1800s. The microscope of those days magnified cells up to 1,500 times. It wasn't until the 1960s and the birth of the electron microscope, which magnifies up to 80,000 times, that scientists were able to see those brain cells at work. Today's electron microscopes can magnify up to 200,000 times. We've come a long way, baby!

By most accounts today, it is generally agreed that an average

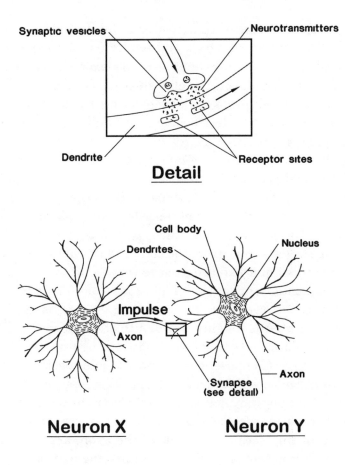

baby is born with around a hundred billion brain cells (give or take a few billion), although some scientists speculate that it could be closer to two hundred billion. At birth, each cell is ready and waiting to be fully developed. Each one hopes to reach the highest possible capacity for human potential through its connections with other cells. A brain cell is called a neuron. Approximately one hundred thousand of these power-packed neurons can fit on the head of a pin. Neurons are the critical actors within the brain and the entire nervous system of the body in the transmission of data or information. Neurons differ from other cells in the body in that they can grow to have upwards of tens of thousands of branches emerging from them. These branches are called dendrites, after the Greek word for "tree." Dendrites receive communications via electrical impulses from other brain cells and send them on to an axon.

Typically, each neuron has only one axon, a long fiber surrounded by an insulating myelin sheath. The myelin sheath is important because it protects the axons from other cells and speeds the transmission of the electrochemical impulses that pass through it. In people with multiple sclerosis, the myelin sheath degenerates and results in eventual loss of muscle control.

In a normal brain, there are tiny breaks along the axon in the myelin sheath that cause the impulses, the action potential, to skip along down the axon at incredible speeds of up to 250 miles per hour. In addition, since there are sometimes tens of thousands of dendrites sending messages to one axon, the cells end up combining and averaging all of this input to one output to send on to the next neuron.

The dendrites and axons of neurons communicate with one another without ever actually touching. There is a tiny area between them that is roughly a millionth of an inch wide. This tiny area, where data is transferred from one neuron to another, is called a synapse. (Synapse is Greek for "to join together.") Normally, a neuron collects information from other neurons through its dendrites. The neuron then sends out electrical impulses through its axon to the synapse. Chemicals called neurotransmitters, which are stored in tiny sacs at the ends of the axon, are then released. They either stimulate or inhibit the connecting neuron. This transfer of data between neurons at the synapse is the magic moment. In its simplest and most basic definition, "learning" occurs when we create new connections between neurons through synapses. The actual process becomes tremendously complex. Simply put, all that we think and feel boils down to trillions of alternating electrical and chemical transmissions between networks of neurons.

Neural Networks

Clusters of neurons that work together are called neural networks. For example, there is a neural network already in place when a baby is born that tells the body to breathe. There is another neural network in place that tells the heart to beat. Babies do not need to be taught how to do these things. However, the vast majority of the thousand trillion possible synaptic connections that a baby's billions of neurons could produce only come together through experience, through stimulation from their environment. For example, language is not hardwired at birth, but when the child hears language, neural networks will form that will ultimately provide the connections necessary to speak. Experience and repetition lend greater strength to these clusters, forming a faster neural network.

Stimulation from the environment holds the key to the cognitive development of the newborn brain and, to a somewhat lesser extent, to the brains of all of us adults as well. The reason for this is that the brain is not unlike most other parts of the body. If we want our muscles to be stronger and bigger, we must stimulate them by lifting weights or challenge them with strenuous activity. If we want our heart to be stronger and more efficient, we must challenge it with aerobic exercise and support it with proper nutrition. Likewise, if we want our brain to be stronger, have more capacity, and operate more efficiently, we must exercise it. We do this by challenging the brain to increase neural networks through exposure to new information from the environment. Building more of these neural networks and building larger, more complex networks earlier in life gives children a broader foundation upon which to build more knowledge throughout life.

Other Important Players

To complicate matters further, neurons aren't the only fish in the sea. It turns out that for every hundred billion neurons, there are at least a trillion cells called glial cells—ten times the number of neurons. Glial comes from the Greek word for "glue," which basically describes what these cells do in the brain: stick to neurons and take care of them. They perform the housekeeping tasks of maintaining a healthy chemical environment around each neuron. They help scavenge debris from injured neurons and act as sponges to clean out excessive toxins of any kind around them. Thus they

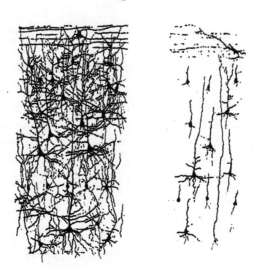

Neural Networks

have become known as the "Cinderella cells."[1] Some glial cells actually wrap around neurons and protect them. Loss of these protective glials can cause gradual paralysis and other symptoms such as those present in victims of multiple sclerosis.

Over the years, other agents have been found to be critical in the balance of normal brain functioning: neurotransmitters. The first neurotransmitter was actually identified around the time of World War I, but scientists were too busy studying how chemicals affected other organs, such as the heart, to worry about how they worked in the brain. The first neurotransmitter identified was acetylcholine. Its importance in our brains is reflected in the fact that this neurotransmitter is deficient in the brains of patients suffering from Alzheimer's disease. Noradrenaline is another neurotransmitter, released in the brain to increase arousal. Drugs such as cocaine boost the availability of this particular neurotransmitter. Noradrenaline is made from a chemical called dopamine. People with Parkinson's disease are lacking in dopamine, while in patients with schizophrenia, there appears to be too much.

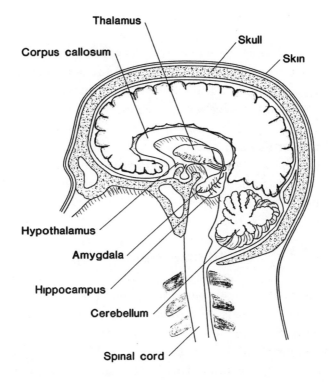

Thalamus

Corpus callosum

Skull

Skin

Hypothalamus

Amygdala

Hippocampus

Cerebellum

Spinal cord

Brain Stem

The oldest part of the brain is the brain stem. This area is located just above the spinal column and is often referred to as the "reptilian brain." It is believed that the brain stem evolved over five hundred million years ago, and eleven of our twelve body nerves that go up to the brain end here. The brain stem harbors the functions of heartbeat, digestion, respiration, and body temperature—functions vital to the survival of the organism. The brain stem is generally believed to be a part of the brain that is hardwired at birth. Thus babies are born with the capabilities to breathe, eat, and excrete without ever being taught how to perform these functions. Those low-level functions are completely controlled and monitored automatically through the brain stem and occur without any conscious effort on our part.

Cerebellum

The cerebellum is located just behind the brain stem and below the back of the cerebrum. This "little brain," as it is often called, coordinates every movement of the body without initiating any of them. Again, the tasks of the cerebellum are automatic; whether we are awake or asleep, it keeps managing our life-sustaining functions. Thanks to the cerebellum, you can usually bring a teacup from the saucer to your lips without spilling a drop. Problems with the cerebellum can result in the inability to coordinate movements as simple as a handshake.

Hippocampus

Hippocampus is the Greek word for "seahorse." This part of the brain was named by early researchers who thought it was shaped like a seahorse, and the name stuck. This little area in the central base of the cerebrum plays a critical role in the functions of memory and learning. It is also critical in the making of meaning. For example, people whose hippocampus is removed or damaged through surgery can remember everything that happened to them prior to surgery but nothing afterward. In fact, without a properly functioning hippocampus, any information coming into memory is lost within seconds. It doesn't stick.

Amygdala

Also possessing a Greek name, this one meaning "almond," the amygdala is a structure attached to the hippocampus. These two small, almond-shaped brain parts play a critical role in decoding emotional messages. When stimulated electrically, the amygdala causes us to feel tremendous fear, rage, or any of a wide range of other aggressive emotions. Recent research suggests that the emotional aspect is a critical one in cognitive learning, which makes sense, since the amygdala is attached to the important meaning-maker, the hippocampus. Additionally, when we recall an experi-ence that was replete with intense emotions, the memory alone can cause us to relive the emotions of the experience. Remember, lovers, they didn't tug at or break your heart, they simply moved your amygdala.

Hypothalamus

This amazing structure has been pinpointed as the brain's pleasure center. It is located just above the amygdala and controls the pitu-itary gland right beside it. The hypothalamus also regulates body temperature, hunger, thirst, and pituitary hormones. Early exper-iments found that by setting up an environment in which rats could stimulate their hypothalamus on their own by pressing a pedal, the rats would do so up to seven thousand times an hour—usually until the point of exhaustion. Some researchers believe that addictive disorders may be related to the dysfunction of this brain part.

Cerebrum

The area that most folks think of as "the brain," that pale gray, wrinkled area that is the first visible part of the brain within the skull, is known as the cerebrum or neocortex. Its weight makes up about 80 to 85 percent of the overall weight of the brain, and it con-trols critical functions such as speech, muscular movement, and thinking and has some role in memory. It coordinates movement with input from the senses. (A different brain area, the basal gan-glia, is involved in more primitive types of movement such as the spontaneous acts of standing up and sitting down.) One large fis-sure spans the top center of the brain, dividing it into two cerebral hemispheres. Contrary to the faulty assumptions of the "left-brain, right-brain" theorists of decades ago, the nerves in the left and right hemispheres do talk to one another. In fact, they are constantly communicating through the corpus callosum, a thick, cable-like structure made up of over 250 million nerve fibers that connects the two halves of the cerebrum. The corpus callosum has more neural connections in it than anywhere else in the entire body. And as mentioned earlier, the corpus callosum is about 11 percent larger in left-handed people.

Since the cerebellum involves interplay between the senses and movement, it is associated with actions that are initially learned, such as driving a stick-shift car. However, once learned, they become almost effortless. Patients who have suffered damage to the cerebellum cannot coordinate complicated sequences of movement and may thus appear clumsy. They find it almost impossible to play a song on the piano or walk in a straight line.

Prefrontal Cortex

This area of the brain, located behind the forehead, is believed to be the most recently evolved area of the brain. The behaviors associated with the prefrontal cortex include imagining, predicting, planning, organizing, and creating. Also associated with this area of the brain are insight, introspection, empathy, reflection, intuitive thought, and formulation of our sense of purpose. This part of the brain houses our most complex thoughts and behaviors and regulates all of our other brain parts. It is believed to develop fully between the ages of twelve and sixteen.

Scientists say that our prefrontal cortex is approximately twice the size that it would need to be for a primate of our size and overall body weight. Since it is the last part of the brain to evolve, it is the most susceptible to environmental factors. And because its development is greatly dependent upon the environment that developed other parts of the brain, and it is arguably the most important body part for high-level critical thinking, much greater attention needs to be given to the development of the prefrontal cortex. There are few studies addressing the early childhood environment and its relationship to the maturation of the prefrontal cortex in the teen years. Research at this point would imply that the level of enrichment in the earliest years directly affects the eventual development of the prefrontal cortex. This is an enormously important area that needs further study.

Damage to the prefrontal cortex can result in a condition called "source amnesia," in which a patient can recall an event but cannot remember a frame of reference for it. An example would be the sensation in dreams of being unable to place experiences into a specific time or location.

The History of Brain Science

The scientific approach to understanding the brain is roughly a century and a half old. Throughout most of civilized history, those curious about the structures and functions of the brain explored every dissectible feature and tried to explain what they found. They were limited to working on the brains of the deceased, since this was the only legal and certainly the only humane way to study what was inside the human skull. Over time, as was customary in the sciences, Latin or Greek names were given to most parts of the brain, thus the terms cerebrum, corpus callosum, hippocampus, amygdala, and so on. Some of the earliest explorers labeled parts of the brain by actual location—forebrain, midbrain, and hindbrain. Only a few decades ago, Paul MacLean explained the brain in relation to the stages of evolution: reptilian, paleomammalian, and mammalian.[2]

The Triune Brain: Reptilian, Mammalian, and Higher-Level Thinking

Explaining brain functioning can be simplified by approaching the brain as three brains in one. Over time, it has evolved, adding ever more mass to the front of the brain as its capabilities have become more and more complex.

As noted earlier, these survival-related activities are controlled by what some call the reptilian brain. This lowest part of the brain, the brain stem, includes no emotion or thinking beyond what is

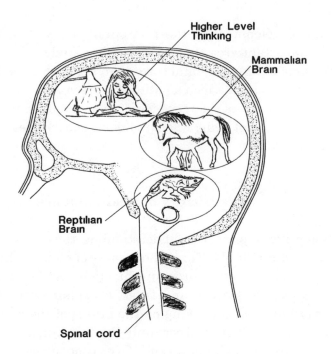

Higher Level
Thinking

Mammalian
Brain

Reptilian
Brain

Spinal cord

The Triune Brain

deemed by it to be necessary to survive. It resembles the functioning of the current brains of reptiles. All processes revolve around physical survival. An appropriate image for the functioning of this part of the brain is a lizard, or perhaps a dinosaur. Eggs are laid and the mother leaves. When the young are hatched, they are basically self-sufficient. They are not dependent upon the mother for survival.

The second section of the brain to evolve was the mammalian brain. This section, also referred to as the limbic system, includes basic emotions that are also linked to survival. If a mammal finds itself starving, there is a fear that survival has been jeopardized. Anger, rage, and emotions associated with that fear arise. One important characteristic of mammals is that (with the exception of the platypus) they do not lay eggs. They give birth to live baby mammals that are dependent upon their mothers for survival. Mammal mothers nurse their young. This is the level at which attachment occurs. The image here is of a mother kitten or monkey with its babies quite literally attached. (Very different from the cold lizard.)

The third section of the brain to evolve was the cerebral cortex. This is the area in which thinking occurs. This thinking can be strong enough even to delay the natural emotions and actions that normally occur with respect to survival. If a young child takes another child's food, the lower-level brain would automatically respond by grabbing it back and perhaps hitting the thief. It is the survival instinct in the lower brain that is triggered and demands immediate action. However, as the brain develops, the higher-level cortical area of the brain can offer the child some options. "There are several considerations for me here. I can ask that child why he took my food and request that he return it. I can go tell the teacher what happened and probably get it back that way. I can look at what else mom has packed in my lunch and determine if I really want that anyway. And tomorrow at lunch, I won't sit near him." The primal concern for survival is subdued and delayed by thought and, ultimately, a plan of action or reaction.

The last area of the brain to develop over time, both evolutionarily speaking and in individual human development, is the prefrontal cortex. This is the area where visualization, planning, imagining, and reasoning take place. This is regarded as the most advanced area of the brain and is not well developed in newborn babies. Many neurologists believe that this area of the brain is largely dependent upon experience for development.

As previously stated, babies arrive in the world already hardwired to breathe, and they are born breathing. We do not have to teach them how. Other functions necessary for survival are also already networked at birth. On the other hand, the vast majority of neural networks in the brain are formed from experience after birth. Babies are born with the capacity to learn to speak a language. In fact, they are born with the capacity to learn all of the languages of the world. However—and this is a crucial "however"—they may never actually learn language if they are not exposed to it in their environment. Language is not hardwired at birth. Furthermore, studies show that babies will learn language much faster and more completely if they are born into an environment in which they hear lots of language.

Clearly, simply studying brain regions and neurons does not begin to tell the entire complicated brain story, which is just in the "once upon a time" stage of revelation. However, the more we know, the more we realize we need to know. And the more parents and caregivers know, the more they will be able to bring all of this exciting research to its place of meaning: their connections with young minds.

Notes

1. Susan Greenfield, *Brain Story* (London: BBC Worldwide, 2000), 32.

2. Paul MacLean, "A Mind of Three Minds: Educating the Triune Brain," in *Education and the Brain: The Seventy-seventh Yearbook of the National Society for the Study of Education, Part 1*, ed. J. Chall and A. Mirsky (Chicago: University of Chicago Press, 1978).

How We Know
What We Know

At birth nearly everyone is programmed to be phenomenal.

—*Barbara Clark,* Growing Up Gifted

Not much more than a decade ago, medical literature on child development reported that the behavior and thinking skills of young children simply "emerged."[1] The brain of the developing child was rarely even mentioned. However, recent technology is making dramatic changes in the way we look at child development.

The last decade has brought incredible technological advances that allow scientists to view the live brain in action. The most startling concept to come out of this research is the vast importance of nurturing the brain properly in the first few years of its life. Positron emission tomography (PET) scans and functional magnetic resonance imaging (fMRI) have catapulted the study of the live brain into warp speed. The remarkable findings from these new techniques occasionally make their way into the headlines, but interpreting these neurological studies is no simple task. In fact, communication between neurologists, psychologists, educators, and parents must be greatly improved if all of this wonderful new information is to become usable.

We know that the earliest brain research took place on cadavers. Many of those studies of brains suggested that there is a direct link between a person's brain and the work that a person does throughout life. As soon as high-powered microscopes allowed us to observe cells and the dendritic branching of neurons, scientists were off and running to prove that changes in the environment alter the communication between cells and consequently change our minds. Studies showed that the more complicated the cognitive demands of a person's particular occupation, the more branches or dendrites were found on that person's neurons over time. In other words, by increasing the complexity of our vocabulary and ideas, we are actually stimulating our dendrites to grow and branch out and changing our brains physiologically.[2]

When a baby is born, most of his or her brain cells have only first- or second-level dendritic branches. The more those cells are exercised, networked, and used in complex ways, the more branches develop along the dendrites. Imagine a tree. The more the limbs branch out, the more leaves will grow and the more shade it will be able to produce. Recent research on Albert Einstein's brain matter revealed seventh-level dendrite branching!

Experience, neural networking, and brain development are directly related and affect each other in physiological ways. Marian Diamond writes that neurologists can now "connect the four-month-old's ability to focus and see at a distance for the first time with the surge of synaptic connections in the visual cortex." Neurologists can also "link the growing coordination between eye and hand movements, like picking up a rattle and bringing it to the mouth, with connections between the visual cortex and its counterpart in the motor cortex."[3] What this shows is that experience begets neural connections, and the more neural connections, the higher an infant's level of activity and behavior.

All Together Now

Perhaps the most important finding of recent brain research is that while we tend to explain parts of the brain and its functioning in terms of regions, those regions are far more involved with one another than had previously been thought possible. No one single brain area is completely responsible for a single mental activity. When mental activity occurs, entire constellations of brain areas are activated at different times, depending on what a person is doing. Consequently, it has become more difficult to pin a precise function to a particular brain part. In addition, we now know that when we build or improve the operation of one area or brain system, it often leads to unforeseen changes in other areas of the brain. Among other things, this may someday help explain the undefined but obvious connection between math performance and music performance in so many children and adults.

Technological Talk: Teachings' Pet

While the brain makes up only a small fraction of our total body weight, it uses up oxygen and glucose at a far greater rate than any other organ in the body. New technology enables us to see just what areas of the brain are using that oxygen and glucose. PET scanning shows in brilliant color which brain areas are most active in burning fuel during different activities. For example, PET scans show a tremendous difference in brain glucose burning between active learning and passive learning. Sitting still, being quiet, and listening to the teacher are almost the equivalent of sleeping when it comes to brain activity. On the other hand, getting up and conducting an interesting experiment reveals activity on the opposite end of the brain activity continuum. Much more glucose is being used when active learning takes place.

Unfortunately, while the PET scan is a phenomenal tool for studying brain activity, the nature of the process limits its use within the medical and scientific community. PET scans involve the injection of a slightly radioactive solution of oxygen and glucose into the body. It is the concentration of the radioactivity that the scanner picks up to portray the colorful image. Because of the risk from this radioactivity, the PET scan is not a technology that can be used indiscriminately to investigate brain activity; it is usually only employed to study patients with severe problems.

Another technological tool, functional magnetic resonance imaging, or fMRI, also monitors brain energy use. This scanner is able to measure oxygen levels in the brain by detecting faint radio signals that are emitted by hemoglobin in the blood, enabling differences to be measured when people undertake different mental activities. An advantage of this technology over the PET scan is that this technique requires no injection of a potentially harmful radioactive solution. But a problem that both the PET and fMRI share is that in terms of brain activity, both are very slow. They tell the brain story in seconds instead of the milliseconds in which the brain really works. Because of the amount of brain activity that can take place over the several seconds needed to produce fMRI or PET scan results, we end up with a somewhat imprecise picture of mental activity, albeit a far better picture than has heretofore been available. Unfortunately, an awful lot of brainwork can be lost in one second!

A third technological tool is the magnetoencephalography, or MEG, scanner. This scanner is an outgrowth of the earlier EEG, or electroencephalography, scan. Whereas the PET and fMRI pick up increased blood flow in parts of the brain that are particularly active, MEG can detect magnetic fields produced from activity around brain cells themselves. Unfortunately, MEG can only pick up signals from around the outer cortex. It loses touch with signals as one tries to look more deeply into the brain. So whereas PET and fMRI are too slow but do show the big picture, MEG shows us the finer tuning but on a much more limited scale. Despite the drawbacks of these three important technological developments, they have greatly advanced brain science.[4]

The act of observing babies in their natural environment, while cumbersome, is still the method of choice for many researchers. The use of videotaping has enhanced this method considerably. However, much of this type of analysis can simply result in highly educated guesswork.

Just what do nonneurologist researchers consider evidence of infant understanding? Most studies assume that infants pay greater attention to some stimuli than to others, revealing their ability to distinguish the difference in the stimuli. Heart rate, breathing, sucking, and visual engagement are the primary behavioral changes that can be observed, helping scientists in their attempts to understand infant thinking. Alan Slater explained in 1994 that for an infant to recognize a new stimulus as different, the baby had to be able to recall the initial stimulus. It has only been since the early 1980s that researchers have recognized infants' ability to develop such memory capabilities. Previously, it had been assumed that infants have no memory ability for this. Once again, faulty assumptions overshadowed our understanding of the infant's complex capabilities.

A Brief History of Psychology

A scientific understanding of the brain and its relationship to the mind and body is very recent in the perspective of the history of man. Advances in the biological sciences around the turn of the twentieth century made it plausible for theorists to suggest that the brain and the mind were, in fact, housed in the same part of the human body, the brain. Prior to this the two were seen as separate and were believed to be found in different and distinct areas of the body. The old view of the mind and heart as separate is reflected in Pascal's famous quotation, "The heart has its reasons which reason does not know."

In the 1600s, philosopher John Locke presented his famous metaphor of the child entering the world as a tabula rasa, or blank slate. Children who, because of their age, operated solely through intuition or emotions were seen as irrational and uncivilized. The younger the children were, the less they were regarded as capable of any intellectual activity. This faulty assumption managed to survive and is still believed by a few educators today, although their numbers are quickly decreasing through retirements and the spread of new knowledge. The blank-slate notion of childhood reasoning is quickly being replaced with developmental research that depicts babies and small children as observant, thinking, reasoning little scientists. "The scientist in the crib" is how the psychologists

Alison Gopnik, Andrew Meltzoff, and Patricia Kuhl suggest that we view infants. To understand how this previous view of babies as a blank slate was established and came to be accepted for so long, we must look briefly at the history of behavior and brain science.

Developmentalism Develops

The prevailing view of babies as unteachable little beings gradually began to change in the early part of the last century. In the 1930s the well-known Swiss biologist Jean Piaget began to record his observations of infants and young children. His subjects were his three children, Jacqueline, Lucienne, and Laurent. The voluminous Piaget diaries record the behavior of his babies in incredible detail. With the assistance of his wife, Valentine, Piaget developed the theory that the baby's world is as highly structured and as complex as that of an adult, just different. The Piagets watched as their babies grew and made sense of their world through experience, enabling them to alter their understanding of reality in a manner, the Piagets argued, that was as natural for them as eating. While Piaget's Stages of Cognitive Development theory was initially ignored, it eventually became well accepted and was incorporated into textbooks in the second half of the century.

The first period of life, Piaget said, is the sensorimotor period, lasting from birth to around two years of age. During this period, a baby differentiates himself from other objects and seeks stimulation. Meanings such as object permanence are defined largely through manipulation of objects. The baby gradually discovers that he is a separate entity from the rest of the world. His hands, feet, fingers, and toes belong to him and are connected to him. Object permanence can be understood by considering a ball rolling across the floor. If the ball rolls under the couch, does it cease to exist? Or is there actually a ball under the couch? One explanation for why many babies appear so fascinated with television programs is the abrupt changing of scenes. Where did those people go? Where did those new ones come from? And how do they fit into that box? The sights seen on a TV screen are illogical to a child in this stage of development (and, many would argue, unhealthy).

An area that Piaget seemed to overlook, however, was the role in child development of adults in the outside environment. Since recent advances in research have proved that environment does matter and we are not simply playing out the blueprint of some genetic plan set at birth, the role of adults in shaping a child's environment becomes critical. While some of the biological changes in a child are caused largely by genetically programmed instructions, even these changes are influenced by, and therefore dependent upon, the kind of care and nourishment that the child receives.

Piaget observed that during the sensorimotor stage of cognitive development, before babies have discovered object permanence, out of sight means out of mind. Piaget suggested that when an older infant continues to look for a ball that has rolled under the couch, this behavior is an indication that object permanence has matured. More recent research, however, suggests that infants as young as three months know that the ball is still under the couch; they simply do not have the motor skills to show us that they know. They may or may not be lacking the memory skills to hold on to the memory of the ball.

Infant Memory

What do you recall from your days in the crib? Probably nothing. Psychologists have termed this state "infantile amnesia." Most people are not able to recall much from their lives before the age of three or three and a half. Sigmund Freud was the first psychologist to attempt to describe this phenomenon. He suggested that infants were probably trying to suppress painful memories. However, his theory seemingly falls apart when we consider that five- and six-year-olds can and do recall terrible experiences without repressing them.

Some researchers have suggested that children younger than five just don't have the neural circuitry in place yet to hold on to memories over a long period of time. But even this theory breaks down in light of more recent research. In 1990, Eve Perris, Nancy

Myers, and Rachel Clifton at the University of Massachusetts found that a six-month-old baby remembered an experiment involving flashing lights and noisemaking toys in their dark lab two years later. In the first experiment, the baby was shown a noisy toy. Then the lights were turned out to see if the child could find the toy by hearing it even though it could not be seen in the dark. The child could. Two years later, in the same lab, when the lights went out, the child reached for the toy, indicating that there was still a memory of the earlier experiment from infancy hiding somewhere in the brain. This astounding finding has been replicated several times since 1992.

Linda Acredolo and Susan Goodwyn, in their book *Baby Minds,* share some fascinating insights gleaned from this experiment. Rather than being afraid in the lab when the lights went out, the two-year-old child that was the subject of this experiment was actually interested in the possible toys to be found in the dark. This observation led Acredolo and Goodwyn to conclude that "by providing children with lots of varied experiences, parents can help them feel at ease in a wider range of circumstances down the line."[5]

So exactly which neural networks are set at birth? In his 1998 textbook, *Psychology,* author David Myers stated, "Researchers believe that Piaget and his followers underestimated young children's competence."[6] Not completely shedding the old paradigm of the blank-slate baby, Piaget did not believe that infants—or even young children before the age of two—could think. More recent research is finding otherwise. The work of Andrew Meltzoff and his colleagues has helped forge the notion that infants are actually discovering their worlds much as scientists conduct research: through constant experimentation and learning from successes and failures. In fact, their research demonstrates that babies come into the world as thinking machines.

Unfortunately, most current authors, including Meltzoff, stop short of drawing the logical conclusion from all of the current data: The failure to provide an enriched environment for babies and young children prevents them from realizing their full potential later in life. It limits their potential to fully develop cognitively and become whatever they care to become in life. It takes away choices they otherwise could have made. In effect, it denies them full exercise of their right to "life, liberty, and the pursuit of happiness."

The Montessori School

One of the most fascinating aspects of studying the past is discovering just how insightful were some of those who went before us, though, regrettably, their genius often went unacknowledged during their lifetimes. Maria Montessori (1870–1952) was one such woman. After becoming Italy's first female physician, she devoted her life to education. In 1907, she opened the Casa dei Bambini (Children's House) in a poor section of Rome. Here she educated the children of beggars, unemployed laborers, criminals, and prostitutes, among others. Her results with their children were so successful that she became quite famous. Unfortunately, her ideas were too far-fetched for the education system of the time. That, and the birth of an illegitimate son, caused her to retreat from the limelight. Though she continued her work and studies with children, by 1920, she was almost forgotten by all but her most fervent followers.

Four decades later, her theories were rediscovered, and today Montessori schools enjoy popularity throughout the world. Basically, the Montessori philosophy of education states that children are eager to master certain tasks during sensitive periods of their development. Maria Montessori worked extensively with retarded children and the developmentally delayed. She found that all children have an inner drive to master tasks; they simply need the appropriate environment and methods to do so. Children do not necessarily want to know what most adults think they should, namely, how to read and write, but they do desire "learning" and need to follow their own interests. Montessori found that children need objects to stimulate their senses and concrete tasks that permit their physical activity and interaction. In her view, the adult's job is rather simple: to be a facilitator of the environment. The adult must be especially watchful for evidence of the child's inner maturation. As this maturation becomes apparent, the adult should simply assist it. For example, if a baby shows a particular interest in a flower while strolling in the park, the adult should pause at the flower to allow the baby to explore it more thoroughly. The Montessori curriculum today includes specially designed manipulatives such as pegs of ascending size to be placed sequentially into appropriate holes in a board. A Montessori classroom typically includes groupings of children of different ages involved in tasks such as pouring from pint-sized pitchers into bowls or cups, folding napkins, and shining shoes. Dolls and trucks aren't typically found in a Montessori classroom. Maria Montessori's studies showed her that young children actually prefer to practice and learn about reality—the activities they see their families engaged in, such as sweeping or cooking. Interest in the fantasy world, she believed, evolved later on.

Entering the Proximal Development Zone

Lev Semenovich Vygotsky was born just three months after Jean Piaget. The son of a banker and a teacher, Vygotsky grew up in a house filled with his parents and seven siblings. The family is said to have loved extensive conversation, and by his teens, Vygotsky was so obviously bright that peers called him the "little professor." He had the misfortune of being born Jewish in Russia in the year 1896 and of only living thirty-eight years. Miraculously, Vygotsky won one of the few lottery spots allocated for Jews to attend the University of Moscow. After starting out in medicine, obtaining a law degree, and then discovering an interest in psychology and obtaining a doctorate in the subject, he discovered that he had tuberculosis. He didn't let this bad news slow him down, however. He proceeded to write seven books and over a hundred journal articles before his death in 1934.

Vygotsky became a professor of psychology. His students reportedly packed the halls to hear what he had to say.[7] Unfortunately, in the late 1930s psychology as a field of study become politicized in Russia and only certain psychologists were acknowledged by the Stalin government. Vygotsky experimented with intelligence tests, and since the Communist Party condemned such tests, Vygotsky's work was suppressed until the late 1950s. Vygotsky had actually criticized IQ tests and was exploring new ways of using them, but this was misunderstood by the authorities.[8] As a result, the West had to wait for a thaw in the Cold War before it could learn of Vygotsky and his fascinating theories. Since the late 1970s, Vygotsky's writings have been available in English translation. However, even though we live in the information age, it still takes time to get the word out when theories such as Vygotsky's emerge. Even today, the majority of books on psychology, educational psychology, gifted education, and related fields fail to even mention Vygotsky's name. In time, however, I believe this astonishing young man's theories of development will change the way the early childhood curriculum is designed.

Vygotsky basically argued that since human development occurs in a particular cultural context, and since that context has such a profound effect on that development, it cannot be explained apart from that setting. For example, some Indian girls in southern Mexico learn extremely complicated weaving patterns at young ages from adults.[9] While outsiders would consider it impossible to perform such complex work at such an early age, the cultural norms of these girls' particular societal setting make it possible. In another tribe, it is common to find men running in excess of seventy miles in a single day. For most cultures, this too, sounds impossible. In Western Europe, most children learn at least two and often three languages by the age of three. A culture that expects more from its children may, in fact, get it.

Vygotsky referred to cultural tools that play critical roles in cognitive development. Some are actual tools (e.g., the printing press) while others are symbolic tools (e.g., our number system). To quote Anita Woolfolk's classic *Educational Psychology,* "Vygotsky emphasized the tools that the culture provides to support thinking. He believed that all higher-order mental processes, such as reasoning and problem-solving, are *mediated* by (accomplished through and with the help of) psychological tools, such as language, signs, and symbols." She goes on to point out that children learn these tools by watching adults in their regular day-to-day experiences.[10]

When we find a text today that references Vygotsky's work, the concept most commonly attributed to him is that of cognitive development as a socially mediated process. Following the Marxist view, Vygotsky believed that human development cannot be separated from its social context. The values, beliefs, and customs of a particular cultural group are transmitted to the next generation through interactions among the adults and the children of that culture and in turn shape everything about the information, including the way in which it is transferred. While Piaget did not consider the direct teaching of adults to be of importance in the development of children in their care, Vygotsky saw the process as critical. In addition, Vygotsky did not accept Piaget's view of the stages of development. He believed that once a child acquires language, the child's much-increased communication ability leads to great and continuing changes in thought processes and, consequently, behavior. He said that without mastering language, a child cannot master logic. Thus, a second principle of Vygotsky is that language plays a central role in the mental development of a child.

Like Piaget, Vygotsky believed that children construct their own knowledge through their experiences; it is not imparted to them. However, unlike Piaget, Vygotsky believed that genuine learning always involves more than one human being. In addition, while behaviorists believe that no structural distinction exists between learning and development, Vygotsky saw a complex relationship. He claimed that learning can actually *lead* development. This is a generally overlooked piece of his theory and is perhaps the most critical with respect to parents and caregivers and the definition of developmentally appropriate practices.

Vygotsky observed and worked with many different groups of children, including the handicapped and children of displaced refugees from very different cultures. He saw that there is a distinct difference between what a child can accomplish unassisted and what a child can accomplish in an environment structured to provide assistance. He labeled the tasks that a child can perform completely alone as the Level of Independent Performance. If a teacher or other adult then intervenes, giving the child a few hints or clues, the second level of performance is the Level of Assisted Performance.

The difference between these two levels of performance he termed the Zone of Proximal Development. He saw that adults could intentionally set up a particular learning environment that would enable children to display knowledge they could not otherwise display.

For example, when asked to count as high as he can, a young child may only be able to count to six. However, if a teacher or adult sets up a row of fifteen blocks and points to each one as the child counts, the child may actually be able count up to fifteen. All that is needed for the higher level of performance is slight assistance from someone who is at the next level; that someone could even be an older child. Consider, for a moment, standardized testing. This type of testing generally tests the individual performance of a child. In the example cited above, which performance best represented the actual knowledge of counting by the child? Clearly the second session revealed his true knowledge. Standardized tests only tell us the first.

Vygotsky found that the Zone of Proximal Development shifts continually in children, and as it moves, children are constantly able to learn more complex concepts and skills. The implications of his theory are that children know more than they can express. *By waiting for unassisted evidence of a particular skill or knowledge to present new knowledge, we could actually be hampering the learning process, slowing it down unnecessarily.* Should a caregiver wait to speak to a child until the child can speak? Of course not. Having the right caregiver with the right assistance at the right time can dramatically change the learning of the child at that moment and consequently change the cognitive development of the child.

On the other hand, boredom has also been shown to affect the brain. In the absence of stimulation, the cortex of the brain thins out. Marian Diamond, in her more than three decades of brain research, has looked closely and extensively at the brains of rats. "A boring environment had a more powerful *thinning* effect on the cortex than an exciting environment had on cortex thickening. Young rats are obviously very susceptible to losing mental ground when not challenged."[11] If this is true for the brains of children as well, it has profound implications for education today. This idea will be discussed in chapter 7.

Windows of Opportunity

In 1977, neurobiologist T. Teyler said, "It has been shown that brain processes present at birth will degenerate if the environmental stimulation necessary to activate them is withheld. It appears that the genetic contribution provides a framework which, if not used, will disappear, but which is capable of further development given the optimal environmental stimulation."[12]

More recent studies have proved Teyler's point. We now know that a baby is born with the capability of learning all of the languages of the world. Unfortunately, after the first six months to a year of life, babies actually lose the ability to hear many of the subtle sounds of different languages that they have not been exposed to in infancy. If the sounds were not present in the infant's environment, the neural circuitry in the brain necessary to hear those sounds does not develop. If the connections within the brain do not form in the first year of life, research suggests that they never fully do. Yes, children and even adults can learn different languages, but it usually takes much longer and they rarely learn the accent of a native speaker. This is because of the failure of the brain to develop the neural networks necessary to hear subtle sounds unique to a language. If, on the other hand, the subtleties of the language are present in the infant's environment, the infant's brain does form the neural circuits needed to hear and speak the language, even if the child doesn't actually take up learning the language until later in life. For example, when many people from Asian cultures learn the English language, they sound out the letter "r" as if it were an "l." "Rice" often sounds like "lice." This is because there is no "r" sound in many Asian languages, and speakers have lost the ability to hear that sound on a neurological level.

Hearing affects the brain profoundly, particularly in the first year of life. Because it affects the organization of the brain, it also affects the ability of a child to learn language and, ultimately, the ability to learn to read. The inability to hear in the first years of life can be a life-altering situation that may not be corrected or compensated for by a greatly enriched environment later on. Unfortunately, it is also the most prevalent congenital birth defect. This represents a window of opportunity and an important piece of evidence in the case for complexity early on. If parents want to enhance children's ability to speak multiple languages more quickly and with minimal or no accents in their adulthood, they should repeatedly expose their babies to the sounds of those languages right from birth.

Research findings suggest that children with hearing impairments, even chronic ear infections in the first two years of life, usually suffer delayed speech and often have other language-related problems throughout their lives, including difficulty learning to read. Hearing, especially in the early years, is critical to the reading process. The brain needs the complex data brought to it through the ears to tool up and lay a foundation for later learning. Different sounds cause the formation of different neural networks. In the absence of sound, those connections do not form.

Jane Healy points out that children with difficulty hearing generally fail to develop fundamental language concepts. Their delayed speech and later reading difficulties can compromise the foundation upon which higher-level thinking depends.[13] Marianne Meyers, a neuropsychologist at the Wake Forest University School of Medicine, states that students who are poor readers in third grade rarely catch up to their peers.[14] Roughly 15 percent of this group drop out of high school. She also says that half of all young adults with criminal records have difficulty reading, as do half of youths with a history of substance abuse. The U.S. Department of Corrections claims that roughly 82 percent of prison inmates do not have high school diplomas, mostly because of reading difficulties. Problems in early childhood can create a lifetime of struggle and certainly a lifetime of unfulfilled possibilities.

This country has had the ability to test the hearing of newborns at birth for several years. Most hospitals have refused to give those tests because of the high cost, largely resulting from the false positives that the tests occasionally produce. Follow-up testing is even more expensive. However, given the known life-changing effects of hearing impairments, including difficulty with learning in school and related social consequences, one may ask if hospitals should be required to give these tests to every newborn. Researchers appear to be unanimous that the earlier the interventions for problems can be carried out, the more the resulting damages can be reduced. Some state policymakers recognize this fact. Fourteen states now mandate hearing tests for all newborns, and others are considering this critical legislation.

Another faulty assumption is that hearing many different languages confuses babies. Some studies have shown that babies hearing two or more languages in their homes occasionally start to speak slightly later than others. However, when they do speak, they are bilingual or trilingual and usually catch up rapidly to the single-language learners. Speech experts guess that the brain is simply sorting out the increased complexity of multiple languages. What is remarkable is the ease with which young children are able to pick up other languages and the difficulty that is encountered when teens try to do the very same thing. By then, the brain is significantly more hardwired and isn't set up for the complex task for which infants are born ready and waiting. Learning a new language after the brain is wired is much like building a skyscraper and, upon completion, deciding to change the plumbing. What could have been accomplished easily at the outset becomes an almost insurmountable challenge later on. Studies of immigrant children learning second languages found that what mattered most was not how long a child had studied the second language but how young the child was when instruction began.

This research has been available for almost a decade. One has to wonder why most school systems continue to ignore it. Typically in the American education system, world-language-acquisition training does not begin until the middle- or high-school years, well past the ideal window of opportunity for learning language. If we genuinely value improved communication and high-level thinking (which is proudly professed by many school mission statements), why do we not mandate second-language learning in the earliest primary grades? Many other countries do this and enjoy a multi-language society.

Linguists such as Steve Pinker of MIT note the evidence of another possible window of opportunity: grammar capacity in children. Around the age of three, children begin to put words together in a meaningful order. However, often pronouns are used incorrectly, as in the statement, "Me go potty." But by age four, most children have picked up enough grammar to correct this to, "I need to go to the potty." Children are able to do this with no lessons on verbs, subjects, prepositional phrases, or sentence diagramming from their parents or caregivers. They come to understand the complex grammar of a language quite naturally—if they hear it.

Evidence of a window of opportunity for grammar comes from children who, for whatever reason—perhaps hearing impairments—are not exposed to proper grammar in their early childhood years. Many of these children are never able to develop correct grammatical structure even with intensive intervention in later years. This even seems to hold true for deaf children and sign language. If these children are diagnosed early and begin to learn sign language before they are six, they become much more proficient signers than children exposed to sign language after the age of six.

A more obvious window of opportunity appears in the study of vision. Neurologists have discovered that synaptic activity for vision multiplies rapidly in two-to-four-month-old babies. This activity continues until around eight months of age. Daphne Maurer of McMaster University in Toronto and psychologist Terri Lewis discovered what happens when the brain is deprived of visual stimuli.[15] In their study involving babies born with cataracts, they found that if the cataracts were not removed before age two, the children would be forever blind in the affected eye. Many of the children in the study were less than seven months old, and in 100 percent of the cases, sight loss had begun before the sixth month of life. In children with a cataract in one eye, neural networks formed normally in the unaffected eye. However, in the case of the other eye, neural networks began forming at birth, apparently expecting to receive data from the affected eye. But when because of the cataract the receptors did not receive data, the dendrites dwindled and the eye's ability to receive data was not able to be restored. According to Jane Healy, if the cataracts were not removed before six months of age, normal vision had little chance of escaping impairment.[16]

Vision develops continuously throughout the first year of life.

The eyes send the data they receive to key cortical areas in the brain, and over time and through interaction with the environment, sight develops. Clearly there is a crucial window of opportunity for the development of sight, and life-altering consequences if the needed stimuli are not present. The good news is that the earlier the problem is detected, the greater the possibility that the child will enjoy normal sight.

What is actually going on in the brains of young children exposed to a rich, stimulating learning environment? Marian Diamond and Janet Hopson, in their wonderful book, *Magic Trees of the Mind,* wrote, "The answer is sculpting the brain by preferentially reinforcing connections within and between certain neural circuits."[17] The more circuits that are strengthened, the more the brain is physically changed. Children who are not exposed to enrichment and are in fact impoverished or abused do not show this brain activity and never catch up to their peers whose neural networks were nurtured.

Whether children have the opportunity to learn correct grammar or multiple languages easily, or whether they have sight or sound at all, may sound like radically different questions. However, they all lead to the same answer. Experience in early childhood affects children's lives in many dramatic ways. Environment in the earliest years matters critically for optimum brain development, whether we are focusing on giving sight to the blind, giving sound to those without hearing, or simply maximizing children's potential.

Notes

1. Marian Diamond and Janet Hopson, *Magic Trees of the Mind* (New York: Plume, 1999), 112.

2. Bob Jacobs, Matthew Schall, and Arnold B. Scheibel, "A Quantitative Dendritic Analysis of Wernicke's Area in Humans. 2. Gender, Hemispheric, and Environmental Factor," *Journal of Comparative Neurology* 327 (1993).

3. Diamond and Hopson, *Magic Trees of the Mind,* 118.

4. Susan Greenfield, *Brain Story* (London: BBC Worldwide, 2000), 23.

5. Linda Acredolo and Susan Goodwyn, *Baby Minds* (New York: Bantam Books, 2000), 65.

6. David Myers, *Psychology* (New York: Worth, 1998), 89.

7. J. V. Wertsch and P. Tulviste, "Vygotsky and Contemporary Developmental Psychology," *Developmental Psychology* 28 (1992): 548–57.

8. William Crain, *Theories of Development* (Upper Saddle River, N.J.: Prentice Hall, 2000), 215.

9. C. P. Childs and P. M. Greenfield, "Informal Modes of Learning and Teaching: The Case of Zinacanteco Weaving," in *Advances in Cross-Cultural Psychology 2,* ed. N. Warren (London: Academic Press, 1982), 269–316.

10. Anita Woolfolk, *Educational Psychology* (Boston: Allyn & Bacon, 2001), 45.

11. Diamond and Hopson, *Magic Trees of the Mind,* 31.

12. T. Teyler, "An Introduction to the Neurosciences," in *The Human Brain,* ed. M. Wittrock (Englewood Cliffs, N.J.: Prentice Hall, 1977), 23.

13. Jane M. Healy, *Your Child's Growing Mind* (New York: Doubleday, 1994), 36.

14. Marianne S. Meyer, "What We Have Learned from Reading Research: Implications for Teaching Struggling Readers" (paper presented at Mineral Springs Elementary School, Winston-Salem, N.C., October 5, 2000), 1.

15. Greenfield, *Brain Story,* 57.

16. Healy, *Your Child's Growing Mind,* 36.

17. Diamond and Hopson, *Magic Trees of the Mind,* 173.

Nurturing Our Nature

Long-lasting effects occur as a result of experience.
The more complex the experience, "the richer" the
environment, the more complex the brain.
— *Richard M. Restak,* The Infant Mind

Researchers estimate that we presently use only about 4 to 5 percent of our neural capacity. They claim that if we were able to fully develop and use all of our neurons, we would be able to process trillions and trillions more tiny pieces of data throughout our lives. But sometime around the age of nine or ten, the brain prunes itself, killing off neurons that have not been used. The conclusion of the brain may be that if those cells have not yet been used, they must not be needed. The brain does continue to grow slightly in size and weight after age ten, but this is the result of dendritic branching, not an increase in the number of cells.

Scientists debate whether or not the pruning process can be slowed or stopped or even whether this would be a healthy prospect for the brain. After all, caterpillars need this process to turn into butterflies. Only time and technology will tell. Meanwhile, the preponderance of evidence from available neuroscience and related research is that if we don't use it, we lose it. We all know this to be the case with other physical capacities. It seems only logical that it would be true with the brain as well.

Children are born with the capacity for speech but don't learn it unless they hear it. To learn speech, children must be spoken to. Parents or caregivers who do not speak to the child in their custody are denying that child the richness of a life with excellent speech and language abilities. And according to Lev Vygotsky, they could be subjecting the child to permanent deficiencies in determining the logic of any matter. Research also shows that the more speech and the more complex speech patterns that the child is exposed to, the more words and more complex speech patterns he or she will learn. The child may even speak sooner than children denied this enrichment. These scenarios are true because of the neural networks that the environment creates in the brain. Learning equates with the building of neural networks, and we can alter the cognitive development of a child by altering his or her environment. Babies learn, and to a great extent their future learning depends on the understanding of the adults in their world that they are baby teachers. We might take issue with Alison Gopnik, Andrew Meltzoff, and Patricia Kuhl's statement, "Babies are already as smart as they can be, they know what they need to know, and they are very effective and selective in getting the kinds of information they need. They are designed to learn about the real world that surrounds them, and they learn by playing with the things in that world, most of all by playing with the people who love them."[1]

Parents who abuse and neglect their children claim to love them. Parents who park their newborn in front of a television set with an educational video, as Classical music plays in the background, represent the other end of the misunderstanding. Humans are complex. Human interaction is the most complex interaction between infants and their environment. Babies will learn from that interaction and, for better or for worse, that learning follows them into adulthood. What do we want them to learn? If they are mistreated by the humans in their environment, their brains will develop differently than if they are not. If their parents or caregivers simply stare at them, their brains will develop differently than if their parents or caregivers talk to them. How the parents talk to them will determine how they themselves will talk. Do we not have a responsibility to see that all children are nurtured in an enriched environment, one in which they can learn more than they will learn lying in a crib in a room with no stimulation whatsoever? Environment matters. It matters because it determines the construction of neural networks. Adults in that environment matter. They can nurture those networks or provide obstacles to their formation. A more complex and richer environment creates a brain with more neural networks, more and better speech abilities, and more and better higher-level thinking abilities. Do we not want this for all children? Do they not deserve this, each and every one?

Genes

All of this complexity is, first of all, based on a genetic blueprint. Genes are located inside brain cells. The genetic blueprint generally determines the organization of the brain and its basic functions. It tells the cells to divide in the first place and sends them on their journey. But even before birth, the complexity and interdependence of the interaction between genes and the environment become evident. Genes may direct cells to divide, but their ability to grow depends on the availability of certain chemicals in their immediate environment. Factors that play a role in how neurons connect to one another and grow in the brain are called epigenetic. An obvious example is the nutritional intake (or lack thereof) of the mother. Smoking, alcohol, and drug use can change the course of the genetic blueprint even before birth. Lack of one or another nutrient can result in serious problems, such as spina bifida.

On a more microscopic level, neurologists have proved that translations of gene messages from DNA to RNA can be different than intended. Some substances, such as hormones, have been found to translate genes differently. Perhaps the most important discovery was Rita Levi Montalcini's remarkable finding of a protein called nerve growth factor (NGF). This important epigenetic substance helps dendrites and axons grow and can also prevent neurons from pruning themselves. This breakthrough won Montalcini the

4

1986 Nobel Prize for Medicine and Physiology.[2]

The pruning of cells from the brain is called apoptosis, a process that is critically important in other forms of life. Tadpoles lose their tails and become frogs through apoptosis. Apoptosis helps caterpillars to become butterflies. Researchers are still studying the apoptosis in the human brain that happens around the age of nine or ten. Some theorize that this pruning not only happens to cells that the brain has not yet used but also to those that the brain believes it will have no more use for in the future. According to Jane Healy, "The brain selectively 'prunes' itself into an efficient information-processing system. . . . Scientists are excited about the finding that the growth of these networks—and thus the ultimate quality of an individual's thought—is responsive to environmental influences."[3]

In an interesting study, Bernard Devlin and his colleagues at the University of Pittsburgh School of Medicine analyzed the IQs of identical and nonidentical twins. They found that identical twins reared apart had similar IQ scores. Initially, the finding was attributed to identical genes. However, after reanalyzing the data from the nonidentical twins reared apart (those with different genes but the same prenatal experience), they found that a significant proportion of the identical twins' IQ scores was actually the result of their common prenatal experience and not genetics.

In addition to all of the research on speech, language use, and sight, it has been found that in the brains of people who are blind and regularly read Braille, larger parts of the areas involved with the sense of touch are developed. In June 1999, a six-year-old boy named Harrison had nearly the entire left side of his brain removed in an attempt to control epileptic seizures. Amazingly, soon after the operation he was able to walk and talk and the seizures disappeared. The miraculous recovery is attributed to the fact that Harrison's brain had compensated for the seizures earlier in his young life. Years prior, the right side of his brain had compensated for the damaged left side.

The human brain is wonderfully plastic. It can adapt by refining and improving and learning within even the most challenging environments. But because the vast majority of studies need to be noninvasive, it is still difficult for neurologists to determine what every change means on a cellular level. In addition, it is virtually impossible to control the environment of humans to determine a cause-and-effect result. Fortunately, research involving the observation of rats has helped greatly to connect environment and neural networking. In particular, the study of "Riley's rats" in the late 1940s helped move the paradigm of fixed intelligence along. Donald Hebb, a Canadian psychologist, found that rats that enjoyed a cage filled with interesting toys and the company of other rats—those who enjoyed the "life of Riley"—had longer dendrites and more neural networks than rats left to a solitary, unstimulating environment. This was evidenced after only four days!

A much more recent study by Dale Purves of Duke University Medical Center in North Carolina found that the cortical areas of rats that involved the sense of touch grew more as they were used more. More important, he found that the enlarged areas used up energy more quickly and had a more extensive supply of blood than other parts of the brain. This was direct evidence that the hardest-working areas of the brain do in fact grow more neural connections.

Beginning before Birth

Evidence has mounted to the point of becoming accepted fact that the prenatal stimulation of babies does make a difference, a positive one. Since the late 1970s, sensitive ultrasound, fetal heart monitors, and fiber optic cameras have helped researchers look at life in the womb more closely. Prior to these technological advances, life before birth was mostly a mystery.

As with early brain science, most fetal studies have been behavioral or developmental rather than neurological in nature. However, the number of neurological studies is increasing, and these studies generally support the theories of the psychologists. Researchers have observed changes in rates of sucking, heart rate, movement, and anything else observable in the fetus. Starting at around six months, the normal fetus can hear, and it is definitely listening. Anthony DeCasper, a psychologist at the University of North Carolina at Greensboro, has studied babies younger than two days old.

Working with colleagues, he invented a device that monitors the sucking of a baby. DeCasper has been able to differentiate a fetus's reaction to its own mother's voice from its reaction to that of a stranger, and the evidence shows that Mom's voice is preferred. Even more interesting, in the first two days of life, an infant would rather hear his or her mother's voice as it sounds in the uterus than as it sounds traveling through the air. The infant would rather hear a recording of Mom's heartbeats than other voices, even Dad's. (Don't worry, Pops, they prefer your voice in a few weeks!) And the infant would rather hear Mom's voice speaking in her native language than anyone, even Mom, speaking in another language.[4] In short, infants prefer what they have become comfortable with or gotten used to. Change represents a challenge, even for infants.

Another experiment by DeCasper showed that the fetus is not only hearing while in utero, it is also learning. He had sixteen pregnant women read Dr. Seuss's well-known book *The Cat in the Hat* twice a day in the last month and a half of pregnancy. After their babies were born, DeCasper used his sucking device to determine the infants' preferences. The babies were read a different children's story, *The King, the Mice, and the Cheese*, and then read *The Cat in the Hat*. Their sucking made obvious that they had listened to, remembered, and preferred the familiar Dr. Seuss.[5]

Further evidence of prenatal learning has come through studies with rats. William Smotherman at Oregon State University taught rats to hate a particular taste and smell even before birth. He injected a small amount of apple juice into the rat mother's amniotic sac and followed this up immediately with a dose of lithium chloride, a substance that causes mammals to become violently sick. Even after the rat pups had been born and were very hungry, they turned and ran from their mothers if her nipples were coated with apple juice. They had clearly learned to associate the smell and taste of the apple juice with the lithium chloride.

Probably the best-known proponent of baby teaching to date is René Van de Carr, an obstetrician in Hayward, California, and founder of "Prenatal University." Van de Carr first came upon this concept in the late 1970s and started teaching classes on the subject in the 1980s. He says he noticed that a fetus reacts quite differently depending on whose hand is laid on the mother's abdomen. He saw distinctly different reactions by the fetus when, say, the mother or father touched the mother's abdomen and then, immediately following, Van de Carr touched the same spot. He was certain that the fetus could detect the different set of hands and instantly froze and stopped responding. It was almost as if the fetus was suddenly asking, "Whose hand is that?"[6]

Van de Carr has claimed for two decades now that the differences in stimulated babies versus nonstimulated babies are "startling! apparent! major!" In behavioral descriptions, the stimulated babies have better muscle control and a better attention span. Their motor capabilities develop faster, speech develops sooner, and they begin verbalizing sooner than nonstimulated babies. The stories from Van de Carr's three thousand patients are intriguing. Most are convinced that the early stimulation produced babies that were more alert, more aware, and more self-confident. Some parents claim their stimulated babies grow to be more sensitive and more polite, have better memories, and are more caring with respect to the needs of others. And all of this comes from stimulation just twice a day for a few minutes. The resounding message from the Van de Carrites is, "If you don't believe it, try it and see for yourself!"

Another study giving evidence of learning in the womb and its lasting effects came from a former music professor at the Eastman School of Music, Donald Shetler.[7] Shetler had been administering the school's Talent Education Program for fourteen years and was interested in finding and encouraging children who showed signs of having musical gifts. He then had an idea on how to generate this gift in the first place. He solicited help from thirty pregnant volunteers, who were willing to play Classical music to their fetuses twice a day for no more than five minutes at a time. The women played the Classical music of Handel or Beethoven in the morning and Bach or some other Baroque composer in the evening with a tempo of sixty beats per minute (the pace a mother's heart generally beats). These women, along with a control group not playing the complex music, checked in with Shetler every six weeks. They then brought their children in to visit him every couple of months for over a decade. During each visit, Shetler interviewed the parents and the children and videotaped their singing or playing.

Shetler found that children stimulated with complex music were talking, on average, three to six months earlier than the unstimulated children. Upon entering school, the stimulated children were further developed in several cognitive areas and many skipped grades in school. Most amazing to Shetler were the musical abilities of the stimulated children. They picked up singing and playing naturally and could memorize musical notes quickly and easily. Shetler is convinced that prenatal musical stimulation heightens and speeds up not only musical abilities but also language skills. He is still in the process of analyzing the hundreds of hours of videotape from his study. Like Van de Carr, Shetler is adamant that he is not trying to create superbabies. "We were trying to see if getting the brain to function at a higher level would enhance a child's chances of reaching his or her fullest potential." He believes it does.[8]

Many researchers, such as Thomas R. Verny, author of *The Secret Life of the Unborn Child*, Beatriz Manrique of Venezuela, and others have contributed to the concept that prenatal stimulation increases cognitive development, language development, hand-eye coordination, and even central nervous system maturity and problem-solving abilities. Manrique, who tracked children for six years, found that the stimulated children averaged fourteen IQ points higher on the Stanford-Binet scale than children who were not stimulated.

Too Much of a Good Thing, or Putting Speed in Perspective

Some people ask if overstimulation should be a concern. Policy number one in medicine is "First do no harm." In utero, normal stimulation appears to do only good. But studies have been conducted with animals that suggest that unnatural interventions could be harmful. For example, researchers in Virginia made small openings in the shells of quail eggs to expose the developing chicks to light to see if they could speed up visual development. Normally, the quail chicks would not encounter direct sunlight until after hatching. Early exposure to light in these cases disrupted the newborn chicks' ability to detect their mothers' movements and they did not follow her like normal quail chicks. It is emphasized that this was an unnatural and developmentally inappropriate invasive intervention.

This dysfunction is similarly represented in problems that some premature babies exhibit. The theory that complex data introduced earlier will enhance neural development in a way that will be evident in more advanced behavior and brain development comes with a developmental component. If babies are born early, they are exposed to much more complex stimuli by the world outside the womb than babies taken to term. Why are they not, then, more intelligent and faster to develop than term babies? The answer lies in the developmental appropriateness of the stimuli. Since the senses do not all come to fruition simultaneously, some senses in premature babies are not ready for the stimulation of the world outside the womb. However, research has shown that developmentally appropriate increased stimulation of premature babies can actually help them considerably. One such area is that of touch. Several studies have shown that premature babies who are stroked and massaged gain weight faster than their peers. In one study, such babies gained 47 percent more weight than premature babies who were not massaged from birth. What happens when a baby is gently massaged? The skin cells send messages to the brain, and the neurons connect in a way that somehow signals other cells to respond. Again, the environment creates the brain activity, for better or worse.

It is important for parents and caregivers to consider conscientiously the issue of when a particular behavior emerges within children and not always assume that sooner means better. Consider the multiple-language learners. The more complex language environment actually causes the brain to take a little longer to hook up the neural circuitry in some cases. However, most would agree that the gift of multiple languages is worth the wait. Albert Einstein barely spoke a word before his fourth birthday!

As is always the case, if parents or caregivers ever have concerns about the development of a child in their care, these should be discussed with the child's pediatrician. In addition, enhancement programs of any kind should only be carried out under the supervision of a qualified children's doctor.

Summary

Nature and nurture work together along a continuum. As Susan Greenfield writes in *Brain Story*:

> In very simple animals, behaviour is more genetically programmed than the product of interaction of the environment. The price paid for this inflexibility is that all the members of a species have similar behavioural repertoire and lifestyle; it seems to us that goldfish, let alone sea slugs, don't come with a wide range of personalities. In animals with more sophisticated brains, however, more emphasis is placed on learning than acting out the mindless dictates of genes. Cats, for example, have far more personality and individuality than goldfish. And in more complex creatures still, such as humans, that shift from nature to nurture is even greater.[9]

The external factors that interact with nature begin even before a child is born. From the perspective of a parent, caregiver, or any other educator, the realization that environment matters critically is of utmost importance for the early years of life. Everything we do and say to and with babies alters their brains biologically and neurologically and ultimately changes their lives. This is an enormous responsibility, not just for parents but also for society. We have the capacity to help build brains that can learn to build their own capacity for learning throughout life. Barbara Clark, an internationally known expert on gifted children, stated: "We have not properly appreciated the ability of our organism to expand or decrease as it interacts with the environment. . . . By the environment we provide, we change not just the behavior of children; we change them at the cellular level. In this way gifted children become biologically different from average learners, not at birth, but as a result of using and developing the wondrous, complex structure with which they were born."[10]

Notes

1. Alison Gopnik, Andrew N. Meltzoff, and Patricia K. Kuhl, *The Scientist in the Crib* (New York: Morrow, 1999), 201.

2. Rita Levi-Montalcini, *In Praise of Imperfection* (New York: Basic Books, 1988).

3. Jane M. Healy, *Your Child's Growing Mind* (New York: Doubleday, 1994), 19.

4. Marian Diamond and Janet L. Hopson, *Magic Trees of the Mind* (New York: Plume, 1999), 87.

5. Anthony DeCasper and Melanie J. Spence, "Prenatal Maternal Speech Influences Newborn's Perception of Speech Sounds," *Infant Behavior and Development* 9 (1986): 133–50.

6. René Van de Carr and Marc Lehrer, "Enhancing Early Speech, Parental Bonding, and Infant Physical Development Using Prenatal Intervention in Standard Obstetric Practice," *Pre- and Peri-Natal Psychology* 1, no. 1 (1986): 20–30.

7. Donald Shetler, "The Inquiry into Prenatal Music Experience: A Report of the Eastman Project, 1980–1987," in *Music and Child Development: The Biology of Music Making, Proceedings of the 1987 Denver Conference,* ed. Frank R. Wilson and Franz L. Roehman (St. Lous, Mo.: MMB Music, 1990).

8. Diamond and Hopson, *Magic Trees of the Mind*, 93.

9. Susan Greenfield, *Brain Story* (London: BBC Worldwide, 2000), 63.

10. Barbara Clark, *Growing Up Gifted* (Columbus, Ohio: Merrill, 1988).

Music Matters

Music is a more potent instrument than any other for education.

—Plato

Throughout this decade of important brain research, the focus has repeatedly been on the significance of the development of the brain in children from birth to age three. A *Time* magazine cover story on February 3, 1997, opened with the sentence "Environment matters." The article went on to report that "of all of the discoveries that have poured out of neuroscience labs in recent years, the finding that the electrical activity of the brain cells changes the physical structure of the brain is perhaps the most breathtaking."[1] It is certainly no secret now that we just can't expose our young children to enough language, love, healthy foods, and all of the wonderfully stimulating experiences that our natural environment has to offer.

More recent research shows us that music matters, too. Listening to it actually causes that electrical activity to occur, resonating within the brain to enhance learning, and probably laying the neural pathways that create a better foundation for learning. Just what is the magic of music? How does it affect us? Our children? Exactly what music is best for babies and young children to cut their teeth on? This chapter and the next address research involving music and its relationship to neural networks. Some researchers believe that selecting the appropriate auditory stimulation for babies and toddlers could be as important as exposing them to language and print—perhaps even more so. The social and emotional effects of music with respect to young children have been well documented. Whether it's a resounding "happy birthday to you" at a party or a solemn hymn in a church, children and adults generally enjoy music and music helps them build a sense of community or social cohesion within a group.

More recently, the cognitive effects of music have been coming to light. The apparent connection between music and math ability is well documented. While this phenomenon is not yet fully understood at a neuron-by-neuron level, empirical evidence reveals that one somehow enhances the other. Other recent studies show that regular exposure to certain types of music may even speed up and enhance language acquisition. In these days of low-cost cassette and CD players, adding music to a child's environment is probably the simplest enriching alteration a parent or caregiver can make. All that is required is strategically placing a playback device in the appropriate area with the appropriate music and pressing a button.

Music and Our Minds

Most people with normal hearing today have seen music performed and heard music played throughout their lives. Music is often referred to as the universal language. It has spanned all cultures throughout known history. There are musical artifacts on the cave walls and in the burial sites of the earliest of civilized man, and it is speculated by some that musical expression preceded speech.[2] Regardless of what language we speak or culture we were raised in, music affects us. Music can make us feel elated or terrified or reduce us to tears, all without using a single word or picture to help elicit the emotion. How does it do this? No one knows yet, but scientists are using all of the wonderful new technology discussed in earlier chapters in seeking an answer to this question.

We have known since the beginning of our knowledge of civilization that music affects human emotions. Emotions, ancient philosophers and thinkers believed, were harbored somewhere in the heart. For centuries, it was believed that the heart and mind were located in different places and were often at odds with each other. Both were considered to be powerful forces, but they were seen as operating separate and apart from each other. It has only been recently that we have learned that it is the amygdala in the brain that holds our heartstrings. So the heart of history past is actually housed in the mind; the two are in fact one. Since music affects our emotions, and since our emotions are lodged in our brains, we can safely conclude that music affects our brains. But beyond the emotional level, how does music affect us? What is music, anyway? How does it differ from speech or other sounds? How does it affect the physiology of our brains?

While studies of the physiological effects of music on the brain are somewhat limited in scope and few in number, there are some that are noteworthy. Most people find that music can bring them pleasure. In 1980, a study was published that gave credence to this feeling on a physiological level. Avram Goldstein injected one group of volunteer listeners with an opiate-receptor antagonist called naloxone. This is a material that covers a pleasure receptor, preventing it from being stimulated. Another group of listeners was injected with saline. After listening to their favorite music, the group injected with the saline reported much greater listening pleasure than the group injected with the naloxone.[3] The implications are that, somehow, music is able to cause the release of endorphins that stimulate the opiate receptors in the brain.

Another study, by Hajaime Fukui in 1996, showed that the testosterone levels of undergraduate students who listened to their favorite music decreased compared to those of students listening to no music. The decrease was apparent proportionately in both male and female students. Since testosterone has been associated with aggressive behavior, perhaps music actually does soothe the savage breast.[4]

Neurophysiologist Walter Freeman suggests in his 1995 book,

Societies of Brains, that oxytocin is released when humans listen to music. Oxytocin is a hormone that is associated with ecstasy and can even have amnesic properties. It is released by both men and women after sexual orgasm. Freeman and cognitive musicologist David Huron offer this property as evidence of how music helps bring about or influence social bonding.[5]

Music Theory 101 for Nonmusicians

We are born with incredible potential for learning. While we are not born knowing how to speak, we are born with the potential to learn language. And many people do learn to speak even though they never learn to decode letters and read or write. Fortunately, throughout history, literacy has been found to be an efficient way to communicate widely. The invention of the printing press dramatically changed society. It changed communication forever and greatly accelerated the need for high levels of literacy worldwide. Society responded. Organized public school systems were set up and laws were passed compelling children to attend. The widespread literacy that resulted not only changed the world, it also changed our brains.

We are also born with the potential to make music. Many people can hum a tune but never learn to decode notes and read or write music. Some argue that reading music is more complex than reading words, primarily because it is so multidimensional. To read words, we need to know the sounds of symbols called letters. The letters appear one after another in groups known as words. Words are grouped to make sentences that are specifically put together to give a meaning beyond what is expressed by a collection of individual words or letters. Words give meaning to letters, sentences give meaning to words. To read music, we need to know both the time values of notes and rests and the pitch of notes. Pitch is whether a note is high or low. So each note in music has both a time element, known as rhythm, and a sound element, known as pitch. There is also a dynamic quality to music that involves whether a note is loud or soft or performed gently or abruptly. "Tempo" is the term for whether a piece of music is fast or slow. Notes are usually orga-nized to form a melody or a musical sentence. To complicate the matter even more, music usually involves several notes sounding at the same time. We never see two or three letters on top of each other, requiring the reader to discern their meaning vertically as well as horizontally, but this is the norm in music reading. Notes added vertically to a melody are generally referred to as harmony. In addition, the musical notes sounding simultaneously often are produced by a wide variety of different-sounding instruments. While in language we hear different-sounding voices, we do not have to decipher language coming from other species. But for the brain to process music, it must deal with the combination of all of these components.

Language and music have an important commonality: both are received and translated by the ear. But the ear hears groups of words and groups of notes differently. If you are in a room filled with talking people, you can only listen to one speaker at a time. You may hear the noise created by everyone talking, but you can only understand or make meaning from what one person at a time is saying. Just try to listen to a nearby conversation when someone is speaking directly to you. A similar sensation results from trying to read an e-mail while talking to someone on the phone. The brain only wants to process language one word at a time. Music, on the other hand, comes at the brain many notes at a time. A symphony orchestra may be playing notes from upwards of forty or fifty dif-ferent instruments, and somehow the ear comprehends it. Some-how the data from these notes reach our brain and, more amazing-ly, our brain understands the message. The groups of notes can excite us, depress us, terrify us, calm us, even in the absence of words.

No one knows yet exactly why this is so, but we do know that to be defined as music, notes cannot just be randomly thrown togeth-er. The notes of music are actually selected to be played together in a very organized way that can be explained by the language of mathematics. Our ears hear sound the way they do because of the vibration of the sound wave. An action or force causes air waves to vibrate. As those vibrating waves reach our eardrums, they are then translated into messages our brain can decipher. A sound wave of molecules bombarding one another is transferred into mechanical energy by the eardrum. This mechanical energy speeds along the auditory nerve and neurons respond. The result is hearing.

Depending upon the number of waves per second in a sound wave, we hear notes as different—higher or lower. For example, the ear hears the pitch A above middle C the way it does because that A vibrates at 440 cycles per second. This is called its frequency. The A note an octave, or eight notes, higher sounds at 880 cycles per second. Consequently, our ears hear it as higher. The more vibrations per second, the higher the note, and vice versa. This matches the length and thickness of the string or pipe or whatever is providing the sound. The smaller or shorter or thinner the string or pipe, the higher the sound, and vice versa.

Other notes sound either consonant or dissonant when played simultaneously with that A because of the mathematical relationships of the vibrations per second of the other notes to the A. Two notes played together form an interval. The combination of the vibrations from each note played together can create in us a sense of rest, or consonance, or it can cause us to feel unsettled, unresolved, or dissonant. For example, a perfect octave (A to A) or a perfect fifth (A to E) played simultaneously on an instrument sounds good or comfortable to us. On the other hand, an A and a B flat do not create that same sense of comfort because of the fraction of their two vibration rates when played together. These mathematical relationships have some bearing on how the ear hears the notes and whether they are heard as pleasant or unpleasant.

Human beings can typically only decipher sound waves between 20 and 20,000 hertz. This represents approximately ten octaves. (A piano keyboard has a little over seven.) Other animals, such as dogs, bats, and dolphins, have a much different hearing range. They can hear sounds that humans cannot. And conceivably, there is an entire "other world" of sound vibrations out there that happens without our conscious hearing realizing it.

A Brief History of Music

Many thinkers have pondered the origin of music and music making. Unfortunately, much of the result remains mere speculation. We do have two notable artifacts to help guide the search. In 1995, a flute made from a bone was discovered by paleontologist Ivan Turk. The flute was found in Divje Babe, Slovenia, in a burial ground roughly forty thousand to eighty thousand years old. It had been devised out of the bone of a now-extinct bear. A wooden flute of this kind would certainly have disintegrated by now. This flute is likely the earliest instrument found to date, but there is obviously no way of determining whether it was the first or five-thousandth instrument actually constructed.[6] Also significant is that this is a tonal instrument rather than a simpler rhythm instrument such as a drum or rattle.

One of the earliest styles of music that we know of is termed monophonic music, mono meaning "one" and phonic meaning "sound." This is simply one melody line of music, usually sung in unison. In the absence of recording devices, the earliest monophonic music that we believe we know the sound of is Gregorian chant. This was music sung by the monks of the early Christian church. Since the monks actually wrote down these tunes in a notation style quite similar to today's and the church kept good records, we are confident of the sounds of these simple tunes. The tunes were collected and codified during the reign of Pope Gregory.

It is worth considering the question of why chanting was so important to monks in the first place. Some believe that before language evolved, our ancestors intoned or sang out their expressions of fear, joy, and so on. Language may now be the expression mode of choice, but we still have "tone of voice," which can define the major message sent in a series of words. And involuntary expressions of varying kinds still erupt oftentimes as simply a sound: "ahhhh" or "mmmm."

According to Robert Gass, author of *Chanting: Discovering Spirit in Sound,* most spiritual traditions believe that the "creation was a manifestation of sacred sound."[7] Chanting may have been our original, natural means of expression. It may help us to achieve an access to God that we could not achieve otherwise. Chanting is still widely exercised today through various religious practices and in activities such as yoga.

Over the centuries, some music became more complex. Polyphonic music ("many sounds") emerged. This was music that included many notes or melodies sounding simultaneously. Some of this polyphony evolved into extremely complicated systematic music throughout history. Early music such as Gregorian chant and much music from the Middle Ages was vocal music. Even much of the music of the Renaissance included instruments only to accompany the vocal lines. Later, however, instrumental music without voices came into its own. In the Baroque era, we find two distinct categories of music: instrumental and vocal. It is also important to note that music was evolving in the East in such countries as China in somewhat different ways. This book focuses primarily on Western music—music that evolved from Western Europe, producing such geniuses as Bach, Mozart, and Beethoven.

Not all music from the past evolved into highly complex polyphonic music. Some songs remained simply a melody with a few accompanying chords to provide harmony. This style of music is generally referred to as homophonic. An example of homophonic music would be a vocal solo with accompanying guitar or piano chords. A more polyphonic texture is created by the singing of a melody in a round, such as "Row, Row, Row Your Boat." Instead of one melody with an accompanying harmony, a round creates a song of many melodies sounding at once.

Some music gained complexity in dynamics or instrumentation but remained structurally simple. Consider the analogy to the Ansel Adams photograph mentioned in the introduction of this book. A detailed black-and-white photo of a tree can be immensely more complex than a black-and-white drawing of a tree by a young child. Both depict trees. Both use the same color scheme. However, in terms of complexity, they are dramatically different.

Cognitive musicologist David Huron has pointed out that as far as we know, the hunter-gatherer societies typically only developed and used rhythm instruments rather than tonal instruments. For example, Native Americans used drums and rattles. The artifacts of the agricultural societies reveal evidence of more complex instruments and more complex music. (We will return to the notion of complexity in music and musical instruments when comparing the music of Wolfgang Amadeus Mozart to that of Johann Sebastian Bach.) We know that Gregorian chant in the early Christian church was unaccompanied vocal music. In a later era, keyboard instruments were added to the Christian liturgical service. At first, only the organ was acceptable, but eventually entire orchestras were incorporated into church music. Music was also used in royal courts. Church music and court music made up the vast majority of music written until the Classical period.

The Classical Period

Although many people refer to any music written before the 1900s as "Classical," music history, like art history, is actually divided into periods based on the specific characteristics or qualities that distinguish it. The years between 1750 and roughly 1830 in the history of music are designated by most musicologists as the actual Classical period of music. This music was quite different from the music in the era that preceded the Classical era, the Baroque, and the music that came after it, Romantic. It not only sounded different, but much of it was used for different purposes. During the 1700s a middle class of people with an increased interest in music grew in size and influence in Europe. Public concerts became popular for the first time, and a few ambitious composers attempted to

Music Era Time Line

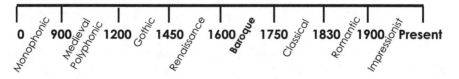

Wolfgang Amadeus Mozart

write music simply for the sake of writing music. Wolfgang Amadeus Mozart was one of the very first. Prior to this, musicians basically had only two career options: work for a church or work for a royal court. "Work" for a musician was defined as either playing an instrument, singing, composing, teaching, or all four. Composers wrote according to the demands of their employer for church services or royal events of some kind.

The general characterization of the music of the Classical period was that of balance and well-organized form. The sonata form became popular for composers. The piano became a popular keyboard instrument, replacing the harpsichord of the Baroque era. Texturally, music of the Classical period generally used the homophonic style of composing, with a clear melody line and supporting harmony. This was true of both vocal and instrumental music.

Today, Mozart is probably the best-known Classical composer. Born into a musical family, he was a child prodigy at the keyboard and grew to discover within himself an adventurous spirit. His music expressed a wider range of emotion than that of composers of former periods. This stylistic difference between Classical music and the music that preceded it, Baroque music, will be discussed in more depth later. Mozart was a keyboard virtuoso, outstanding composer, and the first real "entrepreneur" in the Western musical composition world. By composing music simply for the sake of composing and not always within the framework of an employment request, he was ahead of his time. But he was never quite able to support himself with his craft. He died a pauper and was buried in an unmarked grave in 1791.

> **Well-Known Classical Composers**
>
> *Wolfgang Amadeus Mozart* (January 27, 1756–December 5, 1791) Child prodigy composed a variety of works.
>
> *Ludwig van Beethoven* (December 17, 1770–March 26, 1827) Dramatic composer who lost his hearing later in life but continued to write music. Added choir to his Ninth Symphony.
>
> *Franz Joseph Haydn* (April 1, 1732–May 31, 1809) Father of the string quartet.

The Baroque Period

The era that preceded the Classical period of music in history was called the Baroque period, lasting roughly from 1600 to 1750. During this time, music had begun to take on more organized forms than that of the Renaissance period, which preceded the Baroque. This was the era in which opera became popular. Oratorio, a form of music similar to the opera but for performance in churches, was common. The first orchestras played a form of music called the concerto grosso that later became known as the concerto. Thus, instrumental music without voices came into its own in the Baroque era.

In the Baroque period, for a composer or musician to earn a living at his craft, he generally had to be employed by either the church or some member of a royal court. Other jobs for musicians were scarce, and there were rarely public concerts. Musicians were not rated socially far above servants in those days. However, a few did achieve fame (if not fortune) by writing music and performing it.

Counterpoint

One particular compositional style of writing that became popular in the Baroque period is counterpoint. Very simply put, counterpoint is more than one note sounding together. Recall that Gregorian chant, our best example of monophonic music, was one note or one line of music at a time. In the Middle Ages, polyphony emerged and continued to grow in complexity throughout the Renaissance period. Since the word "polyphony" means many notes or melodies sounding together, this term is often used interchangeably with counterpoint. However, polyphony refers more to a style of music and counterpoint more to a technique. *Grove's Dictionary of Music* says that "polyphony is an end, counterpoint is a means."

> **Well-Known Baroque Composers**
>
> *Johann Sebastian Bach* (March 3, 1685–July 28, 1750) Wrote highly complex music primarily for the church.
>
> *George Frideric Handel* (February 23, 1685—April 14, 1759) Wrote the oratorio *Messiah*.

More specifically, counterpoint is a tightly knit technique for composing polyphonic music that adheres to a strict, comprehensive system of rules. Those rules are ultimately based on mathematical principles since they are, in the most basic sense, driven by the equations of vibrations per second of various pitches of notes and their relationships. The polyphony of the Renaissance was simpler in its design. If you were to listen to a Renaissance vocal song and were then asked to sing the melody, you probably would not be able to recall it. The intermingling of notes, or polyphony, does not involve distinct, recognizable melody lines.

In the Baroque period, however, the melodies of the polyphony became more distinct, carefully designed, and developed so that the listener hears the melody repeated and repeated in a vast array of complex forms while maintaining its recognizability. Some folks today may characterize this complex style of Baroque music as rather unemotional upon first encounter. It has very little dynamic variety. In other words, there is little variation between louds and softs in this music.

Much Ado about Mozart

We know that different music in different styles from different musical eras makes us feel differently. Can it make us think differently? Today, there is evidence that music does affect the brain beyond simply evoking our emotions on occasion. Probably the studies most widely known today are the "Mozart effect" studies conducted in the 1990s.

One study was published in the journal *Nature* in 1993, and *Neuroscience Letters* in 1995. Gordon Shaw, Frances Rauscher, and a group of researchers from the University of California at Irvine released results of a study they had conducted on music and the mind. Specifically, the study involved Mozart's Sonata for Two Pianos (K. 448), a group of college students, and spatial-temporal reasoning. What is spatial-temporal reasoning? It is the intelligence involved in working certain types of math problems, performing some types of music, playing chess, working puzzles, and calculating how to get a basketball through a hoop or a golf ball into a hole. Imagine that you are at the airport. Just how will you get all of those suitcases into the trunk of your car? Your success in this effort depends to a degree upon your own spatial-temporal reasoning abilities. Spatial-temporal reasoning requires the mind to visualize different options in space. It is what enables you to rotate objects or flip them around within your own imagination. It allows you to consider different options for solving a problem by thinking about them before physically trying out the solutions.

In the study, the college students were to be given three sections of the Stanford-Binet IQ test. However, before taking the test, they were divided into three groups. One group observed ten minutes of silence directly before the test. One group listened to easy-listening jazz-style music. The third group listened to ten minutes of the Mozart sonata. According to the UCI study, college students who listened to Mozart's music for ten minuets before taking the IQ test scored, on average, eight or nine points higher than students who listened to the relaxation music or observed ten minutes of silence before taking the test. This study received widespread media attention. The phenomenon from the study was termed the "Mozart effect," largely by the media.[8]

Then in 1997, Rauscher, Shaw, and another team of researchers published the results of yet another study that could be said to involve Mozart's music—or at least so many members of the media thought. In this project, four groups of preschool children were exposed to various stimuli for ten minutes a day over an eight-month period to test for any change in spatial-temporal intelligence. One group had computer lessons, one group had singing lessons, one group had piano lessons (using some simple Mozart melodies as music), and the last group had no lessons. After eight months, no students in the computer lessons, singing lessons, or no-lessons groups showed any significant change. However, the children in the piano lessons group had experienced a 34 percent increase in spatial-temporal intelligence.[9] A detailed discussion of these studies is found in Shaw's book, *Keeping Mozart in Mind*. A CD of Mozart's Sonata for Two Pianos is included with the book.

Soon after the release of the first study, two major recording companies produced and marketed CDs designed to boost test scores. Advertisements included phrases like "Mozart makes you smarter" and "Hum your way to an A" under titles such as *Mozart for Your Mind*. The second study coincided with unusual media attention to the outpouring of research on babies' brains, and entrepreneurs rushed in to capitalize on applying the concept of the Mozart effect to young children. The crafty entrepreneur who beat Shaw to the U.S. Patent and Trademark Office and secured the use of the phrase "the Mozart Effect" had nothing to do with the studies. Only a couple of pages in his book, *The Mozart Effect*, even refer to the study. With respect to the second study, few stopped to ask what Mozart music the three- and four-year-olds were actually mastering in their piano lessons and whether those little melodies ("Twinkle, Twinkle Little Star") were really the determining factor in the change in spatial-temporal reasoning. (Mozart wrote a wonderful theme and variations on the popular tune "Twinkle, Twinkle Little Star" for the piano. It was common at the time to take well-known melodies and compose music around them.) Few reporters appeared to consider the possibility that it was the hand-eye-ear-mind combination that was responsible for the change in the preschoolers' spatial-temporal reasoning, not Mozart's melodies. After all, how much Mozart could a normal three- or four-year-old really master?

The point is, music is made up of patterns and relationships, and listening to complex music and learning to perform music improves spatial-temporal brain performance. In an interview with the *Chicago Tribune* on May 24, 1998, Shaw is quoted as saying, "We first started working on a model of the brain that represents how we might think and reason. Music was the last thing on our minds. Physicists look for patterns and relationships. Our model was based on the idea that groups of neurons formed networks and that these networks eventually involved the whole brain."

Additional research has shown this to be true. The Mozart Effect study with listening has been replicated many times over with many more successes than failures. Also, more and more evidence shows connections between math ability and music as well as language-acquisition networks and music-listening networks within the brain.

More recent studies have confirmed that piano lessons do dramatically improve spatial-temporal reasoning in elementary-school-age children, whether or not they use Mozart melodies as the repertoire. Some school districts in the United States that can afford it have already mandated piano lessons in their K–5 curriculum and others are considering movement in this direction.[10] Much evidence suggests that music training develops mental flexibility in adults as well, strengthening the cognitive connections between music and other learning throughout a lifetime.[11]

Is It Mozart or Is It Music?

Since the Mozart Effect studies, researchers have taken a closer look at data they already had compiled involving music and the brain and found many definite connections. It is necessary, however, to insert a word about research and babies at this point. As discussed in previous chapters, there are many different kinds of research, and research on babies is especially complicated. Behavioral research involves observing behaviors. With respect to babies, we are basically talking about sucking, breathing, heartbeats, and eye movement. Neurological research involves observing the activity of neurons within the brain and physiological changes in the brain to help discover how the brain learns and what strengthens the brain's operating capacity. This relatively new field of study is called cognitive neurology.

Many different types of research are going on simultaneously, and results can vary depending upon the interpretation of the data. The reader is cautioned to think carefully about the reports before drawing the same conclusion that, say, a marketing company might draw. On the other hand, drawing broad general conclusions from some research is criticized even when the outcome seems obvious.

For example, according to a study conducted by the National Center for Abuse and Neglect, 66 percent of institutionalized delinquents—offenders under the age of eighteen years of age, most of whom never go on to become hardened criminals—had a history of abuse and neglect. This information comes from a profound book, *Licensing Parents*, by Jack Westman. The author makes a powerful case for considering early interventions of a more radical nature, including mandating parenting licenses before adults are allowed to take babies home from the hospital. After all, we need a license to drive, a license to teach, a license to build buildings. Which of these is more important than raising our children? According to other research, over 90 percent of full-fledged prison inmates had a history of abuse and neglect as young children.[12] Now, on the basis of these data, can we say that child abuse and neglect create criminals? No. But can we safely deduce that it is probably not a good idea to abuse and neglect children? Yes.

Clearly there is plenty of research revealing that there are strong links between abuse and neglect in childhood and achievement later in life. However, there has been no study that I know of that has set up two groups of babies, nurtured and provided one group with an enriched learning environment, abused and neglected the other, and then checked back twenty years later to see which group had the most members grow up to become prison inmates. Hopefully, this study will never have to be conducted for us to conclude that abuse and neglect of young children can have disastrous effects. But without this type of study, how do we know for sure that this is true? As in other fields, much of the study of music and the mind at this point is just this type of research. Some of it is after the fact and thus is easily criticized as not proving conclusively that music helps improve the brain.

Consider the following studies. According to the Educational Testing Service, high school students with course work and experience in music performance and music appreciation scored higher on the Scholastic Assessment Test (SAT). These scores were fifty-one points higher on the verbal and thirty-nine points higher on the math test for music performance only, and sixty-one points higher on the verbal and forty-six points higher on the math test for music performance and appreciation compared to students with no music participation. It certainly appears that students with music training perform significantly better on the SAT than students without such training. But who can say for certain whether or not it is the music training itself that causes the higher scores?

The February 1999 issue of the *National Association of Secondary School Principals Bulletin* includes an article giving further evidence of the music-achievement connection. Records of medical school applications show that 66 percent of music majors who applied to medical school were admitted. This was the highest of any group, including biochemistry majors, of whom only 44 percent were admitted. The same issue of the publication points out that nations whose students consistently outperform the United States in tests assessing science achievement are the countries where music is a primary focus of the curriculum. In Grant Venerable's 1989 book, *The Paradox of the Silicon Savior,* he states that one of the most striking facts in Silicon Valley industry is that "the very best engineers and technical designers are, nearly without exception, practicing musicians."[13]

The crown jewel of the music-mind-achievement connection for educators came on August 29, 2000, when the Harvard Graduate School of Education released the results of its Project Zero study. This meta-analysis, which included a comprehensive synthesis of 188 different studies, found convincing connections between music training and academic achievement. The researchers said they found three areas in which "clear causal links could be demonstrated between the arts and achievement in a non-arts, academic area." These were listening to music and spatial-temporal reasoning; learning to play music and spatial reasoning; and classroom drama and verbal skills.

What about cognitive neurological studies? First, the Mozart Effect studies showed changes in spatial-temporal reasoning resulting from listening to and performing complex music. However, it should be noted that when the college students listened to the Sonata for Two Pianos, that improvement in spatial-temporal reasoning only lasted a matter of minutes. For a change to be considered long-term, it must last more than twenty-four hours. The piano-lesson studies with the young children were able to accomplish this.

Gottfried Schlaug, a Harvard Medical School neurology instructor, used magnetic resonance imaging (MRI) technology to examine the brains of musicians who took up their instruments before the age of seven, those who began later than seven, and nonmusicians. He found that certain regions of the brain, specifically the corpus callosum and right motor cortex, were larger in musicians who started their musical training before age seven. MRI was also used to find that musicians with perfect pitch have larger left temporal lobes than nonmusicians do.[14]

Susan Greenfield, in her outstanding work, *Brain Story*, states, "Expert violinists have a greater cortical area devoted to their left fingers than the rest of us, but they are not born this way—regular practice has stimulated the cortex to form complex new connections." She goes on to point out that "more than any other animal, we depend on experience—not genes—to give us the skills we need to survive. As we evolved and our brains became larger, the ability to form more neuronal connections, and hence to form more associations, gradually increased."

Drawing on our evidence from prior chapters on the impact of the early environment on a child's brain, we know the following: Babies can hear even before they are born. The hearing sense comes to fruition between twenty and thirty weeks' gestation in the womb. We also know that what a baby hears can wire or rewire the brain for better acquisition of language skills and possibly other skills. We could conclude, then, that listening to complex music and ultimately learning to interact with music needs to happen as soon as possible in a child's life. Therefore, we know that listening to complex music in infancy, as with speech, wires up the child's neural circuitry.

Clearly music affects more than simply our emotions and our SAT scores. Sometimes music rewires the brain and somehow improves learning. Will any music work? Perhaps not. Some studies indicate that the music must be complex. Singing simple children's songs daily was not found to improve brain functioning in Shaw and Rauscher's study.

In a more recent study by Shaw and a large team of researchers, a Music Spatial-Temporal (MST) Math Program focused on teaching proportional reasoning, fractions, and symmetry to second graders. These important concepts are sometimes introduced in the second grade in American schools but are not studied in detail until the fourth or fifth grade. In their study, the researchers used the MST math curriculum to teach 380 second graders from urban schools these complex skills. After completing the curriculum, the children performed at the same level on the Advanced Math Concepts Test as fourth graders from a higher-socioeconomic school who did not have the training. In addition, the second graders increased their scores on California's Stanford 9 math test dramatically (www.MINDinst.org).

Shaw points out that our current education system concentrates on two basic types of reasoning. One is language-analytic reasoning skills. An example of this linear type of reasoning would be solving an equation to get a quantitative result: two plus two equals four. The second type of reasoning is spatial-temporal. An example of this reasoning would be playing chess, in which the players have to be able to think several moves ahead and consider multiple possible solutions for variable problems. It requires mental imagining within the brain. Shaw and many others have observed that the education system spends the vast majority of instructional time, particularly in early elementary grades, teaching language-analytic reasoning skills. Shaw argues that it is spatial-temporal reasoning that is critical to developing the skills needed for mathematicians and scientists and, somehow, music helps the brain gear up for this type of thinking.[15]

Peter Perret, conductor of the Winston Salem Piedmont Triad Orchestra, decided that if young children could not come to the symphony, he would take the symphony to them. His objective was to test the theory that music training increases brain performance in some way. He selected a local elementary school made up of economically disadvantaged children; 70 percent were on free or reduced-price lunch. Perret and musicians from the orchestra met with Bolton Elementary School principal Ann Shortt and teachers from the school and together they designed a program now known as the Bolton Project.

The principal began piping Classical music through the school intercom system into the halls, library, and lunchroom. A group of orchestra members became resident musicians at the school, working three hours a day, three to four days a week, for sixteen weeks over three years. They did more than simply play complex music for the students; they worked with teachers to integrate music throughout the curriculum and taught music reading and skills. At the end of the third year, when the students involved in the study took the state standardized tests to measure math and reading competence, a full 85 percent tested at or above their grade level in reading and 89 percent in math. The year prior to the music infusion program, only 40 percent of students were at grade level. The staff, students, parents, and orchestra members are convinced it was the music learning and listening program that helped boost the school's performance. There was, however, no control group in this study. Every child was given access to the enrichment. Perret was not interested in publishing contracts in this experiment, just helping children learn. However, an article describing the study in more detail appears in the January-February 1999 issue of *Symphony: The Magazine of the American Symphony Orchestra League.*

Another series of studies with control groups shows that music training may, in fact, enhance both types of reasoning to which Shaw referred. In 1996, Martin F. Gardiner, a visiting scholar at the Center for Study of Human Development at Brown University, studied first-grade classes using the Kodály method of singing training. Six first-grade classes were divided into two groups. One group had regular classroom music and art instruction. The other group had Kodály method singing training. This method involves singing songs that are sequenced in complexity. The Kodály method uses solfège (do, re, mi) syllables to identify pitches and also includes hand and arm movements for each pitch of the scale. As the children master each song, the complexity of the next song is increased. After seven months, students in the Kodály group performed the same or better in reading but "zoomed ahead of their peers in math, even though they had started out slightly behind."[16] This was true of children in low, middle, or top achievement groups in their prior kindergarten classes. Gardiner stated, "If you develop one kind of mental skill involved in one area of learning, the brain can at least sometimes make learning easier through transfer." This study also shows that singing simple children's songs daily may soothe the soul but may not do much, if anything, to stimulate synapses. Only by continually increasing the complexity of a task do more complex neural networks form.

In the early primary years, children must learn that the number one comes before two, two before three, and so on. The Kodály method of learning through singing that "do" comes before and is lower than "re," and "re" comes before and is lower than "mi," helps build a neural network that comprehends the concepts "less than" and "greater than" but involves the added complexity of higher and lower. It gives another dimension to the task. It involves more complex neural networks.

Clearly, listening to complex music and learning to play or sing some kinds of music affect the brain in a way that can enhance performance, particularly in the area of mathematics. No one yet knows exactly why this is so on a neurological level. We have seen that music can somehow affect the direct release of oxytocin and testosterone in the brain. How do notes and differing patterns of notes actually do this? How do they stimulate neurons to connect? Future technological advances are likely the key to the secret relationship between complex musical sounds and the math ability that they clearly enhance. Fortunately, researchers like Shaw and Gardiner are working on unlocking these secrets.

Notes

1. James Collins, "The Day-Care Dilemma," *Time,* February 3, 1997, 58.

2. David Huron, "Music and Mind: Foundations of Cognitive Musicology" (lecture 2 of the 1999 Ernest Bloch Lectures at the University of California at Berkeley, September 24, 1999). Available at http://dactyl.som.ohio-state.edu/Music220/Bloch.lectures/Bloch.lectures.html [accessed October 12, 2000].

3. Avram Goldstein, "Thrills in Response to Music and Other Stimuli," *Physiological Psychology* 8, no. 1 (1980): 126–29.

4. Huron, "Music and Mind."

5. W. J. Freeman, *Societies of Brains: A Study in the Neuroscience of Love and Hate* (Hillsdale, N.Y.: Lawrence Erlbaum Associates, 1995).

6. Huron, "Music and Mind."

7. Robert Gass with Kathleen Brehony, *Chanting: Discovering Spirit in Sound* (New York: Broadway Books, 1999), 59.

8. Frances Rauscher et al., "Listening to Mozart Enhances Spatial-Temporal Reasoning: Towards a Neurophysiological Basis," *Neuroscience Letters* 185 (1995): 44–47.

9. Frances Rauscher et al., "Music Training Causes Long-Term Enhancement of Preschool Children's Reasoning," *Neurological Research* 19 (1997): 2–8.

10. Karen Abercrombie, "Wisconsin District Requires Piano Lessons for K–5 Students," *Education Week*, October 14, 1998, 3.

11. James R. Ponter, "Academic Achievement and the Need for a Comprehensive, Developmental Music Curriculum," *NASSP Bulletin*, February 1999, 108.

12. Sharon L. Kagan, keynote speech at Kindergarten Readiness Conference, Winston-Salem, N.C., October 21, 2000.

13. Ponter, "Academic Achievement," 108–13.

14. Debra Viadero, "Music on the Mind," *Education Week*, April 8, 1998, 25.

15. Amy B. Graziano, Gordon L. Shaw, and Eric L. Wright, "Music Training Enhances Spatial-Temporal Reasoning in Young Children: Towards Educational Experiments," *Early Childhood Connections* (Summer 1997): 30–36.

16. Martin Gardiner, "Effects of Arts on Learning," *Nature* 384 (May 26, 1996): 192.

The Bach Effect

*What is this? Now, there is something one can learn
from!*

> —Wolfgang Amadeus Mozart
> upon hearing Bach's double-chorus motet,
> Singet dem Herrn ein neues Lied

In 1756 a baby boy was born in Salzburg, Austria. The boy was
named Johann Chrysostom Wolfgang Gottlieb Mozart and was
called Wolfgang. Wolfgang's parents were both musicians. Daddy
Leopold, in particular, was well known as a violinist and composer
and leader of the local orchestra. Wolfgang also had an older sister,
Nannerl, who showed remarkable talent as a musician at an early
age. Nannerl was five years old when Wolfgang was born. Leopold
was her music teacher. So infancy for Wolfgang was spent in a crib
surrounded by the sounds of the music of the time, from his father's
composing to his mother's singing and his sister's rigorous harpsichord lessons.

Thanks to a 1984 Academy Award–winning film, *Amadeus*, we
all know quite a bit about Wolfgang Mozart's life—for example,
that he was considered a child genius and began playing the harpsichord at age four and composing his own pieces by age five. This

movie helped catapult the adult life of the child prodigy into a household story for millions. The name Amadeus is the Latin version of one of Mozart's middle names, Gottlieb, which translates as "loved by God."

Why Mozart? (A Personal Story)

My mother and father had an old piano in the garage when I was born. I showed interest in it at around five or six years old. So my parents began piano lessons for me in second grade. Thanks to several wonderful teachers along the way and the tenacity of my parents, I became a rather accomplished pianist, performing a Mozart piano concerto with my junior high school orchestra and later winning a young artist's award for piano in high school. I loved playing and singing, and while my talents in piano far exceeded my singing ability, I loved the choral experience and decided to become a choir director. My first university degree was in vocal music education, and I taught music for ten years.

I had heard somewhere long ago that playing Classical music for young children was "good" for them in some way. I had never researched why this was believed, but it felt intuitively right. Each night when I gave my young daughter, Leigh, her bath, I played Classical music for her. And since I knew the history of music, I was playing *real* Classical music for her, that is, music written roughly between the years 1750 and 1830.

A little later, through my work in high school administration, I had become aware of the Mozart Effect research before it was even published. I recall attending a workshop for principals at the University of California at Irvine and hearing one of the other administrators mention it in passing. Some of the students in the study were at his school. I called lead researcher Gordon Shaw immediately, and he was kind enough to send me information on what had taken place to that point. Since I had already been playing Mozart for Leigh, I thought to myself, "Aren't I the clever mommy?" But one morning when Leigh was almost two years old, I woke up and wondered, "Why Mozart?" Why did Gordon Shaw and Fran

Rauscher select the music of Mozart for their studies? What was so magical about the music of Mozart?

I proceeded to do what I thought any good mom would do: I called the researchers themselves on the telephone. When asked why they used Mozart's music in their studies, the researchers responded, "We chose Mozart since he was composing at the age of four. Thus we expect that Mozart was exploiting the inherent repertoire of spatial-temporal firing patterns in the (brain's) cortex."[1] In layman's terms, the researchers were wondering if listening to the Classical music produced by the mind of the phenomenal child prodigy, Wolfgang Mozart, would have an effect on the brain of the listener. Could Mozart's complex music, specifically the K. 448 Sonata for Two Pianos, alter or enhance brain performance in some way? (For a much more in-depth, neurologically based explanation of this phenomenon, see Shaw's personal account in his book, *Keeping Mozart in Mind*.)

Perhaps it is relevant that these researchers were not primarily musicians or education specialists. They were neurologists, assisted by a psychologist who had played cello. But having been a music teacher and education professional, and especially being a new mom, I wasn't as interested in what was coming out of the mind of Mozart as about *what was going in*!

Mozart Wasn't Raised on Mozart

Wolfgang Mozart was not listening to Wolfgang Mozart as he lay in his crib in 1756. In fact, it was not Classical music at all that he was hearing from birth to age three, it was Baroque. Exactly what Baroque music? It was most certainly highly complex, mathematically organized Baroque counterpoint that he was hearing in infancy. This was the standard music pedagogy of the day. Mozart's older sister practiced it daily on the harpsichord. It is likely that his father's other students practiced it at their lessons. We know that Amadeus was literally surrounded each and every day by Baroque-style music. This systematically developed Baroque music surely helped to build connections in the mind of the child genius in his first three years of life. Because Mozart had a brain that possessed genius potential, this music stimulated his mental development to such a point that he began playing music at four and composing soon afterward. And as any trained musician can tell you, Baroque music is quite different from Classical in many significant ways. The Baroque period is characterized by much greater emphasis on the organization of the vertical combinations of contrapuntal melodies in conjunction with major-minor tonalities to produce complex harmonic, rhythmic, and textural structures and expression. It is brain music and appeals to the intellect over the emotions. (Bach enthusiasts would argue that the intellectual stimulation brings emotional pleasure.)

The move from this Baroque counterpoint to Classical music was actually a move away from a high level of complexity and toward simpler harmonies. According to the *Harvard Dictionary of Music,* Classical composers "wished music to be developed in forms which should be more the free inspiration of the composer and less restricted in their systematic development." The move away from this Baroque counterpoint to Classical music was actually a move away from a high level of complexity and toward simpler harmonies. According to *The New Grove Dictionary of Music and Musicians,* this was necessary to satisfy the musical tastes of the new phenomenon of an emerging middle class of concert goers in the Classical Era. "Among the most striking features that distinguish harmony after about 1730 from that of the Baroque Era [is] the slowing down of harmonic rhythm. . . . It was necessary if the tonal outline of larger-scale form was to be accessible to a public comprising more ordinary music lovers than connoisseurs."[2] The Oxford Companion to Music states, "The phase that followed (the Baroque Period) was one of resimplification. In the music of Bach's sons, Haydn, Mozart . . . and others of that period, we do not find the complex polyphonic network of Bach. . . . Even Mozart, who greatly admired what he knew of the works of Bach, did not often emulate their depth and complexity."[3]

The dramatic differences in textures of the music in the Baroque and Classical eras could have been the result of other changes, including changes in the technology of the musical instruments themselves. The primary household keyboard instrument of the Baroque era was the harpsichord. The pianoforte ("piano" meaning soft and "forte" meaning loud) began to come into wider use in Mozart's day. The pianoforte, now just called the piano, could play louder or softer music simply by variations of touch on the part of the performer. The mechanics of the Baroque harpsichord prohibited any dynamic changes from the touch of the performers' fingers. As a key on the harpsichord's keyboard was played, a quill plucked the string in the instrument's body. Whether the performer touched the key lightly or firmly, the plucking of the string was the same, causing the dynamic level of the note performed to be of one level.

The new instrument, the pianoforte, made it possible to produce varied volumes of notes within a single piece of music. In a piano, when the performer strikes a key on the keyboard, a hammer hits the string to cause it to vibrate. If the performer touches a key lightly, the hammer inside the body of the instrument lightly hits the string and a soft sound is created. If, however, the performer increases the force with which the key is played, the hammer's force is increased and the sound of the note generated is louder. This offered performers, and consequently composers, the ability to create music with much more dynamic variation. This single technological advance accelerated the move away from the intellectually appealing Baroque music and toward the more emotional appeal of Classical and Romantic styles of music. While the piano reached its true legitimacy as an instrument at the hands of Beethoven (1770–1827), Mozart (1756–91) played and composed for the piano. Some sources state that he was the first to do so and that Mozart played the major role in popularizing this new instrument in Europe.

Leopold knew that he had something special on his hands with young Wolfgang. Combining the talents of this child prodigy with the hottest new instrument on the market was sure to create a sensation throughout eighteenth-century Europe. Whether to take advantage of the situation or simply to share the uniqueness of his boy wonder, Leopold took Wolfgang on the road at an early age. (Leopold is often criticized today for this; some argue that these grueling road trips may have affected Wolfgang's already fragile health and contributed to his early death.) Regardless of the reason, Leopold took him and his sister, Nannerl, to perform for the masses, and they were a sensation.

Much to the dismay of Mozart-worshipers, Leopold and Wolfgang suffered from a credibility problem. Because Wolfgang was a child performer, his advertised age was frequently a year or two younger than his actual age.[4] Since he was a sickly child and was much smaller than other children his age, this was easily believable. In addition, Leopold was known to "help" Wolfgang with his early compositions.[5]

When Wolfgang was eight years old, his performances on the pianoforte were spectacular. However, Leopold realized that his son's initial compositions were "less than spectacular."[6] While he could play anything he heard or saw, writing wasn't Wolfgang's forte early on. Leopold moved the family from Paris to England in 1764 for several reasons, one of which was for Mozart to study counterpoint. It was here that Wolfgang met his most beloved and influential mentor, Johann Christian Bach, the youngest son of the great Johann Sebastian Bach. Mozart scholars, including Teodor Wyzewa and Georges Saint-Foix, agree that "John Christian Bach became the only, true teacher of Mozart."[7] While this may sound a bit overblown, since obviously his father and sister had a tremendous impact on his musicianship, musicologists generally agree that five months under the close tutelage of J. C. Bach transformed Mozart's composing abilities.

In his book *The Mozart Handbook,* Louis Biancolli calls Mozart's early compositions "far from mature and sometimes positively faulty. There can thus be no doubt that the sonatas and symphonies of this period were extensively revised by Leopold, and some possibly by J. C. Bach. It does not, surely, detract from the miracle of the genius of a child approaching his ninth birthday to admit that he must have been helped in committing his ideas tidily to paper. What matters is that he did have ideas."[8] However, throughout Mozart's life, he frequently incorporated the work of his father, Bach, Handel, and an undeterminable number of other composers into his works. There are "startling similarities" between

Johann Sebastian Bach

many of his symphonies and those of J. C. Bach.[9] However, this was not unusual in a time when printed books of music were a luxury, concerts were scarce, and tape recorders and CD players were nonexistent. Composers regularly borrowed others' work, sometimes to pay tribute, at other times to improve on another's composition. In the case of J. C. Bach, Wolfgang was paying tribute. In his letters to his father, he repeatedly expressed his love for his mentor. On the other hand, he also "improved" upon some of Antonio Salieri's work.

A Bit about Bach

For over two centuries, the Bach family produced a long line of successful musicians, so much so that the Bach name became synonymous with professional musicianship, as seven generations were "actively musical." Johann Sebastian was of the fifth generation. The *Oxford Companion to Music* states that "38 [Bachs] were known as eminent musicians but of the great majority of these, no music survives and of many of the others only 2 or 3 compositions are available in print."

As each new generation was born into another music-filled home, the Bachs' competencies and artistry escalated, reaching their peak with the complex work of Johann Sebastian Bach, or Papa Bach. Two of J. S. Bach's sons, Philipp Emanuel and Johann Christian, actually became more famous during their lifetimes than their father, but this could be attributed to the change in status for musicians that came about during the Classical period. Johann Sebastian was known in his time more as an exceptionally talented organist than as a composer.

Over the last two centuries, however, appreciation of Bach's talents as a composer has grown steadily. This was largely due to the efforts of great musicians like Felix Mendelssohn who recognized Bach's genius and began to spread the word about it. The *New Bach Reader* states that Mendelssohn "worked zealously and successfully for the cause of Bach" in the 1800s. Robert Schumann also repeatedly invoked the name of Bach. His often-quoted advice was, "Play conscientiously the fugues of good masters, above all those of Johann Sebastian Bach. Let the *Well-Tempered Clavier* [of Bach] be your daily bread. Then you will certainly become a solid musician. . . . We are never at an end with Bach, how he seems to grow more profound the oftener he is heard."

According to *The New Bach Reader,* "What is true of the monumental proportions, the contrapuntal intensity, the rhythmic consistency of Bach's works is just as true of the cogency of his themes, the expressiveness of his melodies, the force and richness of his harmony, the diversity and logic of his orchestration. In all of them he brought seeds well germinated by his predecessors to fruition on a scale undreamed of before him."[10]

The *Harvard Dictionary of Music* notes that the contrasting style of true polyphony not only persisted but reached its very acme of perfection and greatness at the hands of the Baroque period's best-known composer, Johann Sebastian Bach. The *World Book Encyclopedia* says he is "considered the greatest genius of Baroque music" and "the musician's musician." Richard Wagner claimed that Bach's works are "the most stupendous wonder in all music." Gioacchino Rossini stated that "if Beethoven is a prodigy among men, Bach is a miracle of God." Johannes Brahms claimed that the most important event to take place in the world during his lifetime was the unification of Germany. The second most important? "When all of Bach's surviving works were finally published."[11] No musician has been regarded by those in the field as more brilliant than J. S. Bach. *The International Cyclopedia of Music and Musicians* states, "It's hardly too much to say that he is the greatest musical genius the world has ever known."[12]

Fortunately, we have much evidence of Johann Sebastian Bach's brilliance today. This was largely due to his teaching. The typical teaching practice of the time was for beginning students to spend their first few years of study copying manuscripts. Bach wrote many works strictly for this purpose. These were circulated widely, and it is possible that Mozart was first exposed to Bach's counterpoint through these types of manuscripts. Leopold and Nannerl Mozart may have used them for practicing. In addition, Leopold's duties as the town music master included Sunday church services. Counterpoint prevailed in the church services of this time and well into the Classical era. It is likely that young Mozart heard this music regularly at church on Sundays as well.

We don't know a lot about Bach's personal life, as he didn't write many letters, in contrast to Mozart's hundreds. However, he was referred to as a solid citizen. He was a hard and dedicated worker and probably didn't have time to write much beyond his vast library of musical works. There is no doubt that the focus of Bach's life was spiritual—specifically, providing music for the services of the churches where he worked. He was a pious Lutheran and completely devoted to his duty to God, writing and performing music.

Melody by Bach

We have addressed monophonic music, that is, one line of melody without accompaniment. Polyphonic music is many melodies played together. To help with our comparison of Mozart's and

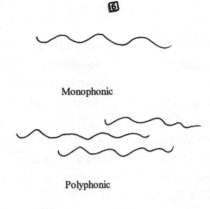

Monophonic

Polyphonic

Homophonic

Bach's music, we need to bring homophonic music into the discussion. Homophonic music is typically a melody line with an accompanying harmony of some kind. In homophony, there is clearly one important melody and the rest of the music simply supports or reinforces or highlights that melody. In contrast, polyphonic music involves at least two or more melodies of equal importance. The song is the development or working out of the different melodies in part and in whole. The three textures of music may be represented visually.

Bach's counterpoint was unusually complex. According to *Grove's Dictionary of Music,* what other composers "saw realized in exemplary fashion in the music of Bach was the idea of music at once contrapuntal and full of character, at once strict and eloquent: Music in which the characteristic and the eloquent features of a contrapuntally differentiated texture were not forced on it from outside but were actually generated by it." Bach's fugues and fugal passages probably represent the best and most complex counterpoint compositions ever created. However, whether he was composing the giant B minor Mass or Two-Part Inventions for the Keyboard, Bach's work shows an attention to detail and genius in every respect.

The Art of Fugue

By the time Wolfgang Mozart was in his mid-twenties, we know that he was collecting the fugues of J. S. Bach. In a letter to his father in 1782, he reported that every Sunday he went to Baron van Swieten's house at noon to hear Bach's music performed. He then arranged five of Johann Sebastian's fugues from *The Well-Tempered Clavier* and *The Art of the Fugue* for strings. In his letter to his sister dated April 10, 1782, he wrote, "I am collecting at the moment the fugues of Bach." Then on April 20, 1782, he referred to the fugue as "this most artistic and beautiful of all musical forms." His first fugue was written for his beloved wife, Constanze. He wrote to his sister again:

> I wrote down a fugue for her. So that is its origin. I have purposely written above it Andant Maestoso, as it must not be played too fast. For if a fugue is not played slowly, the ear cannot clearly distinguish the theme when it comes in and consequently the effect is entirely missed. In time, and when I have a favourable opportunity, I intend to write five more and then present them to the Baron van Swieten, whose collection of good music, though small in quantity, is great in quality. And for that very reason I beg you to keep your promise not to show this composition to a soul. Learn it by heart and play it. It is not so easy to pick up a fugue by ear. If Papa has not yet had those works by Eberlin copied, so much the better, for in the meantime I have got hold of them and now I see that they are unfortunately far too trivial to deserve a place beside Handel and Bach.[13]

Mozart was not alone in appreciating the genius of J. S. Bach. In March of 1783, a magazine article about eleven-year-old Beethoven reported that "he plays most of *The Well-Tempered Clavier* by Sebastian Bach, which Mr. Neefe has placed in his hands. Anyone who knows this collection of preludes and fugues in all the keys (which one could almost call the *non plus ultra*) will know what that means."[14] Douglas R. Hofstadter's lengthy, Pulitzer Prize–winning book, *Gödel, Escher, Bach: An Eternal Golden Braid,* shows how extraordinarily complex yet meaningful patterns can arise out of seemingly meaningless symbols. Hofstadter's examples of the ultimate depiction of these complex patterns include Gödel, a brilliant mathematician; Escher, a unique and fascinating artist; and J. S. Bach—specifically, his fugues.

Exactly what is a fugue? Answering this question for nonmusicians is no simple task. Let us begin with a canon or a round. A melody is devised which, by nature of its very construction, can be played with itself at later intervals within the song. The simplest examples of canons would be "Row, Row, Row Your Boat" and "Frère Jacques." A more complex canon would be one in which the main melody is repeated on a follow-up entry varying not only in the place where it enters and its rhythm but also in its pitch. For example, when the main theme comes in for the second voice, it may enter on a different note instead of the identical note of the main theme. If the first note in "Row, Row, Row Your Boat" is C, the second singer may come in on a G instead. In this more complex form of canon, the harmonization of the tune remains the same, but different notes or harmonics are used.

Canons get more and more complex as the construction of the main theme gets more complex to accommodate the increased complexity. For example, instead of the second (or third or fourth) voice coming in simply on a different pitch, it may come in on a different pitch and be accelerated in rhythm or diminished in speed or augmented. Bach even wrote some themes that could then be played upside-down and backwards and still work to harmonize the main theme. A good example of music in which most of these complex examples show up in the fugal sections is the *Musical Offering*. Many consider this Bach's most outstanding accomplishment in counterpoint.

A fugue is very much like a canon. It has a theme that recurs in different melodies or voices at different speeds and in different forms throughout the work. (The words "voice" and "melody" are used interchangeably, as most of Bach's fugues are not actually sung but are played on instruments.) It is somewhat less rigid than the canon, as it allows for free voices and some slight departures from the exact theme. A fugue typically begins with a single voice or single line of music followed soon thereafter by a second voice of the same theme, only in a different place or different form. The original subject continues as a countersubject to the second voice of the first. As the main theme is developed in all of its possible variations, the countersubject voices, exempt from the strict copying of a canon, continue expressing and developing whatever the composer wishes.

The key is in the exorbitantly complex designs of Bach's melodies. For a melody to be manipulated so extensively within the fugal passages, its structure must be completely intentioned from the start to lend itself to such complexity. Bach didn't just write out a melody of which he liked the sound. He engineered it so that it could be developed into a complex fugue.

In the *Musical Offering*, we find Bach presenting canonic puzzle after canonic puzzle in the fugal form. Bach's students worked hard to try and solve them. Bach even wrote in one section, "quaerendo invenietis" (by seeking, you will discover). One of Bach's pupils, Johann Philipp Kirnberger, did solve the canon puzzles. However, Hofstadter wonders whether there could be even more solutions left to seek.[15] Bach's genius in complex composition seems to extend beyond mortal capabilities.

Bach included no dynamic markings on his solo keyboard or organ works. It was not the style of the day to do so, probably because it was not yet possible to get dynamic variation within a piece of music. Markings such as "crescendo" and "decrescendo" did not come into use until Jommelli used them in Mannheim, Germany, much later. Bach used complexity of texture to express himself through his composing, not emotional louds and softs.

On the personal side, Johann Sebastian was truly the embodiment of what many now refer to as "family values." He was an exceptionally spiritual man, a devoted Lutheran, and he was employed as a church musician almost all of his long life. To Bach, whether music was sacred or secular, it had only one purpose: to honor God.[16] Bach inscribed the initials "J. J." at the beginning of many of his compositions. This stood for "Jesus jova," or "Jesus help." He closed most of his writing with the letters "SDG," which stood for "Soli Deo Gloria," which translates as "to God alone be the glory." Bach dedicated some of his keyboard works to Jesus, even though they were not composed for a church performance.

Performers of Bach's vocal works often report a sense of spiritual transformation upon their completion.

A dedicated father, Bach had twenty children, ten of whom lived to adulthood, which was normal for this time period. Bach's first wife died after the birth of the fourth child. His second wife was a soprano in his church choir. Several of his children became musicians, and of those, we know that two had contact with Wolfgang Mozart. In fact, Mozart said of Carl Philipp Emanuel Bach's music, "His is the parent and we are the children" (*Oxford Companion to Music*). Bach's devotion to family and God cause him to be something of an anomaly among Mozart, Beethoven, Tchaikovsky, and many of the other great musicians.

Bach's music has steadily grown in stature over the decades. It was even included aboard *Voyager 1* and *2* as examples of the best that human culture has to offer. J. N. Forkel referred to Bach as "the greatest musical poet and the greatest musical orator that ever existed, and probably ever will exist."[17]

Building Brains with Bach

All of this knowledge of music and music history, combined with my intuition as a mother and educator, was not enough for me to completely jump with both feet into a Bach-versus-Mozart debate. Even though I had performed many works by both composers over the years and knew that Bach fugues were light-years more complicated for me to memorize and perform than Mozart sonatas, I was looking for more. I wanted specific research that showed that the increased complexity of Bach's music could be exhibited in building brainpower in people who played and heard it. Clearly it affected the Bachs themselves. The Bach babies who listened to their music generation after generation grew into an unusual number of gifted musicians and, later, doctors and lawyers. But could this have been genetic? From what we know today of the influence of environment on the developing brain, I thought not. We know now that practice doesn't make perfect, it makes permanent! However, I decided to research the theory further. I decided to study the history of giftedness and see if there might be some enlightening information there.

There was a lot, and yet there was nothing. There was plenty of evidence that gifted musical children became exceptional achievers, and vice versa. There was also a great deal of information to support the enriched childhood environment as a major contributing factor to giftedness. However, in trying to differentiate between the music of Mozart and the music of Bach, I repeatedly ran into that familiar error: lumping all music written before 1900 into the category of "Classical." I found statements such as the following:

S. [names are protected in the texts] liked only Classical music performed by experts and had no interest in the music of contemporary composers. . . . He had no language before age 5 but was able to hum songs he heard on the radio or phonograph from an early age.[18]

N. P., an only child, had entered a residential home for long-term placement at age 17. He had almost no spontaneous speech, made little eye contact and displayed the obsessive and bizarre behavior patterns characteristic of autism. . . . He gave local concerts of popular music, hymns and his favorite, Classical pieces.[19]

[Erwin's father] reported that his son tried to sing before he was 1 year old; before 2, reproduced tunes correctly . . . by 9, he learned Beethoven sonatas and Bach fugues after hearing them three or four times.[20]

Where did Erwin hear Bach fugues? His father was a musician with the Royal Opera Chorus in Budapest. The point is, there are stories of the profound effects of music on gifted children. Unfortunately, the differentiation I was looking for between specific styles of music was not apparent.

Almost as if led by the spirit of the Old Wig (as his sons called him) himself, I was able to come serendipitously upon support for my theory. Waiting in a doctor's office, I picked up an issue of *Vogue* magazine. It opened right to a story on a brilliant young pianist, Evgeny Kissin. The reporter writing the story shared an interesting statement by his mother:

> A few days later, at a reception for his twenty-first birthday, I was able to meet his mother and his teacher, Mme Kantor. They were both a good deal more talkative, and as immediately recognizable as characters out of a Broadway show. "I knew Genya was talented at the age of two," his mother tells me. "His older sister was practicing a Bach fugue at the piano. And Genya just started singing it the next day. I asked him to do it again, and he could."[21]

Like Mozart, this young genius was hearing the complex counterpoint of the Baroque era in his crib. Who but me would have picked up the significance of the song Genya was hearing? Or there is the *60 Minutes* broadcast on December 29, 1996. Lesley Stahl interviewed concert violinist Martha Curtis, who suffered from severe epileptic seizures. Often the seizures would attack in the middle of a symphony performance. Over the years, the medications she had tried were becoming less and less effective in warding off the seizures. In 1991, she decided to undergo risky surgery on her brain to try and remove the origins of the seizures without removing her ability to play music. Surgeons removed part of her right temporal lobe, an area usually associated with interpreting and memorizing music.

As soon as Curtis came out of intensive care, she asked for her violin so she could find out if her life's love could be continued. What did she play? "I played unaccompanied Bach, because that's the hardest stuff (to play) from memory." Again, who but me would pick up that a musician's ultimate test on her own brain would naturally involve the complex music of Bach?

Back when I called Gordon Shaw to ask why he used the music of Mozart in his Mozart Effect studies, I posed this question: "What about Bach?" He told me that he did not consider himself a musician and that any complex music would probably achieve a similar result. I then called another of the researchers, Frances Rauscher, and asked her the same question. Having been a concert cellist at one time, Rauscher answered with the same response—hesitation—and then, "Any complex music would probably do."

You can imagine my delight when after years of considering this concept, Shaw included the following suggestion in his new book, *Keeping Mozart in Mind*: "Perhaps the question most asked is what other pieces of music will yield the enhancements in spatial-temporal reasoning generated by the Mozart Sonata (K. 448)? (We suggest trying the highly structured music of J. S. Bach.)"[22]

And in fact, serious researchers today are taking his advice. At the Institute for Music Research at the University of Texas at San Antonio, Don Hodges and his team are studying the neural networks used for processing music. Very little is known today about how this is done in the brain. Their study is designed to determine the brain areas that are activated by melody, harmony, and rhythm. They are accomplishing this by having musicians listen to Bach chorales with intentional errors implanted. In one experiment, the error is in the melody. In another, it is in the harmony, and in a third, the error is in the rhythm. While the results are not all in, at this point the researchers can say, "It is clear that there is no 'music center' (in the brain) and it is also clear that music does not happen only in the right side of the brain."[23]

Other studies are planned at the Institute of Music Research, and so far, it is the music of Bach that is being used. When I asked Hodges why the researchers chose Bach, he answered that it was the result of the symmetry and organization. They felt it would most clearly depict the results they were looking for. This type of research will eventually help us see why music affects learning the way it does, why math performance is enhanced so by some music, and why spatial-temporal reason is so enhanced by listening to complex music. How music works in the brain and its role in the learning process need much more serious study.

Going for Baroque

Mozart is considered a Classical composer. But the music that built the brain of this young genius was not Classical, it was Baroque.

The sounds he heard repeatedly, even before birth, were his older sister practicing counterpoint on the harpsichord and his father's violin students fiddling away at the highly structured, systematic Baroque sounds of the day. And that music was not merely repetitive. It represented the ultimate in melodic development in a complex way.

We hear musical sounds the way we do because each note vibrates at a different frequency. Simply put, music can be explained mathematically, and the relationship between tones is a mathematical one. Exposing infants from birth to age three to the highly complex contrapuntal music of the Baroque era can remarkably improve the learning potential, creativity, and resulting intellect of the child later in life. This is especially true if listening to complex music in the crib is followed up with consistent music lessons in the early years. This music enhances neural activity between brain cells. Case study research reveals much evidence of Baroque musical exposure producing "geniuses" at early ages.

Unfortunately, many neurologists and sociologists lump what they refer to as "complex music" into the era of Classical music without recognizing the critical differences between the musical eras that affect children's development. Throughout decades of studies of gifted children, when musical factors are considered, these factors are repeatedly labeled and reported in a category referred to as "Classical"; today we have no way of determining if this was specifically music written in the late 1700s and early 1800s. The Classical music of Mozart is brilliant and should be the standard listening curriculum in the primary grades. However, listening is developmental. Johann Sebastian Bach's contrapuntal compositions are to the music world what Ansel Adams's black-and-white photographs are to the visual art world: extraordinarily complex, but developmentally appropriate for babies and young children.

Early childhood music clinicians throw around the phrase "developmentally appropriate music making" as though it were defined somewhere and set in stone. It is not. Some aspects of a possible definition are obvious. Clearly children naturally engage in musical activity to help give meaning to experiences or to express themselves. Music can also provide an opportunity for connecting socially to other children and adults. Making music is an fine example of active involvement and has been shown to enhance memory skills. Many three-year-olds who cannot recite the letter names of the alphabet can easily sing them in the classic ABC song, "Tell me what you think of me." Likewise with numbers: "One, two, buckle my shoe." Many parents use musical tunes to teach their toddlers those critical pieces of information that they may be too young "developmentally" to recall: their full name, phone number, and address. In this respect, music is used to speed up what may still be considered developmentally inappropriate. Yet children can do it and apparently enjoy doing it.

Music is made up of patterns. When children internalize different kinds of music, they are not only building connections between the rhythm and melodic and dynamic patterns of the songs, they are making other connections as well. Unfortunately, we do not yet know how this occurs. What we do know is that music and math skills clearly go hand-in-hand, and music and memory have some special association as well. Music may even prepare the brain for all learning.

Superlearning

In 1979, Sheila Ostrander, Lynn Schroeder, and Nancy Ostrander published a book entitled *Superlearning*. In it, they claimed that there was a way to learn how to learn better, develop "super memory banks," and speed up learning in general. They cited in particular the work of a Bulgarian researcher, Georgi Lozanov, who had observed outstanding results in helping people achieve a state of relaxed alertness. In this state, the body is relaxed but the mind is alert and especially susceptible to taking in and retaining new information, such as learning a language.

Music was found to be a critical element in achieving this special state of mind. While the authors repeatedly use the terms "Classical" and "Baroque" interchangeably, Lozanov is quoted as emphasizing that the music has to be a special kind of Baroque music, with roughly sixty beats per minute, the approximate number of heartbeats in a minute. Lozanov also said that string instruments produce better results because of the higher frequencies of the pitches. Most of the music recommended by Lozanov and the authors was written by J. S. Bach.

While there were no neurological studies then available to help defend their case, the authors do point out that using a particular style of music to achieve a particular state of mind is certainly not an entirely new concept. They share the well-known story of Bach's composition of the "Goldberg Variations." As the story goes, Russian envoy Count Kayserling had a bad case of insomnia. When he would awaken in the night, he called for the musician Johann Goldberg to be awakened so he could play "that song" for the count yet again. What song? Goldberg played a piece on the harpsichord that had been specifically written for Kayserling by J. S. Bach to help with his sleeplessness. It was "calm, yet bright." Shortly after Goldberg would begin to play, the count would find himself feeling restful and soon would be able to fall back to sleep. He even had Goldberg placed in a room near his own bedroom to be ready to play this wonderful healing music immediately upon request. The count was so pleased with the effects of the song that he gave Bach a generous gift of gold. The song was named the "Goldberg Variations" in honor of the poor, obliging harpsichordist.

Lozanov is quoted as claiming that he is quite sure the great composers, philosophers, and poets from ages gone by were well aware of these special musical powers and used them unabashedly. *Superlearning* goes on to promote hypnosis, parapsychology, the development of intuition, and even extrasensory perception.

In 1994, the three authors published a follow-up, *Superlearning 2000*. While their work has been criticized by some as being a bit overblown and far-reaching—suggesting we can accomplish a year's worth of learning a new language in only three days—no one has criticized the authors' choice of Baroque music for achieving the "superlearning" state. *Superlearning 2000* contains page after page after page of testimonials of the success of the authors' method. It says that over two hundred centers have been set up worldwide to use *Superlearning* methods to learn and heal.

In *Superlearning 2000*, the music references are more specific. The authors state that the music definitely needs to be a specific type of Baroque music with between sixty and sixty-four beats per minute: "Test showed music scored for string instruments rich in harmonic overtones produced superior results to music scored for brass, horns or pipe organ."[24] Again, the music of J. S. Bach is cited repeatedly in testimonials claiming greatly increased learning, the curing of learning disabilities in young children, and the healing of just about any ailment known to man. These stories present a compelling case for listening to Baroque music to enhance thinking.

In *The Secret Life of the Unborn Child*, Thomas Verny claims that it is easy to tell what kind of music the fetus enjoys listening to: Baroque. "Put Vivaldi on the phonograph and even the most agitated baby relaxes. Put Beethoven on and even the calmest child starts kicking and moving."[25] Unborn babies might not understand words, but somehow they understand tone and tone of voice. They seem to prefer soft, soothing sentences from their mothers, no matter what the words are, and Baroque music with no words at all.[26] Verny suggests that these sounds make babies feel comfortable, loved, and wanted even before they are born.

Listening and Learning

If we acknowledge that simply adding some types of music to the environment helps the brain learn better and in some instances faster, then perhaps music should be mandated in standard curriculums. And if simply listening to a particular style of music helps nurture neural networks and, in turn, helps the brain function better, why would we view exposing infants to wonderful complex music any differently than providing proper nourishment for a baby? We want our babies to be physically healthy. Why? Is the answer any different than the reason we want our babies to be mentally and emotionally healthy? The point is, parents who want to provide the best environment for their babies' brains and bodies desire this for the same reasons they do not feed them candy bars, potato chips, or soda pop. They love their children and want them to be healthy and happy. They are not trying to create Michael Jordans or Cal Ripkens. They are not trying to create superbabies or tiny Einsteins. They simply want to maximize their children's God-given potential in every domain.

Where is the line between providing only for a child's minimal survival needs and child abuse? In the motives of the parents? Is "developmental appropriateness" that which is needed for children's survival? Or is it what we know from research to be best for enhancing their cognitive development? Until scientists can give parents and caregivers a clear definition of what is not just good for enriching a child's development but what is best and what is detrimental, we will continue to have parents and caregivers conducting the vast majority of research in this critical field by trial and error.

NAEYC

The National Association for the Education of Young Children (NAEYC) is an organization, founded in 1926, that is dedicated to promoting high-quality, developmentally appropriate programs for all children and their families. The organization's website (www.naeyc.org) states:

> *Developmentally appropriate practices* result from the process of professionals making decisions about the well-being and education of children based on at least three important kinds of information or knowledge:
>
> 1. what is known about child development and learning—knowledge of age-related human characteristics that permits general predictions within an age range about what activities, materials, interactions, or experiences will be safe, healthy, interesting, achievable, and also challenging to children;
>
> 2. what is known about the strengths, interests, and needs of each individual child in the group to be able to adapt for and be responsive to inevitable individual variation; and
>
> 3. knowledge of the social and cultural contexts in which

children live to ensure that learning experiences are meaningful, relevant, and respectful for the participating children and their families.

In an effort to be somewhat more specific, NAEYC has also outlined the principles of child development and learning that inform developmentally appropriate practice. They are:

1. Domains of children's development—physical, social, emotional, and cognitive—are closely related. Development in one domain influences, and is influenced by, development in other domains. . . .

2. Development occurs in a relatively orderly sequence, with later abilities, skills, and knowledge building on those already acquired. . . .

3. Development proceeds at varying rates from child to child as well as unevenly within different areas of each child's functioning. . . .

4. Early experiences have both cumulative and delayed effects on individual children's development; optimal periods exist for certain types of development and learning. . . .

5. Development proceeds in predictable directions toward greater complexity, organization, and internalization. . . .

6. Development and learning occur in and are influenced by multiple social and cultural contexts. . . .

7. Children are active learners, drawing on direct physical and social experience as well as culturally transmitted knowledge to construct their own understandings of the world around them. . . .

8. Development and learning result from interaction of biological maturation and the environment, which includes both the physical and social worlds that children live in. . . .

9. Play is an important vehicle for children's social, emotional, and cognitive development, as well as a reflection of their development. . . .

10. Development advances when children have opportunities to practice newly acquired skills as well as when they experience a challenge just beyond the level of their present mastery. . . .

11. Children demonstrate different modes of knowing and

learning and different ways of representing what they know. . . .

12. Children develop and learn best in the context of a community where they are safe and valued, their physical needs are met, and they feel psychologically secure.[27]

If "developmentally appropriate" means appropriate for developing the brain to achieve its inborn capacity, a maximally enriching environment is critical. The principles upon which the accepted definition of "developmental appropriateness" is founded do not conflict with the notion of increasing the complexity of stimuli in the crib and beyond. Take another look at principle 10. This principle appears to represent Vygotsky's theory of the Zone of Proximal Development. Children who interact with those more capable than they—for example, their parents or more capable siblings—develop knowledge, attitudes, and ideas from these interactions. The learning is dependent, then, upon the quality or complexity that is present in their environment. For example, the more complex the language present, the more complex the language learned. The more languages present, the more languages learned. The more complex the music present, the more complex the foundation laid for future learning, and in some cases, as with the Bachs and Mozarts, the more musical abilities learned. Since music is known to translate into improved mathematical ability and spatial-temporal reasoning, the more complex music present, the more complex mathematical understanding can be expected later on. Something not yet thoroughly understood in listening to complex music helps set the stage for more complex learning.

So exactly what is developmentally appropriate? It must depend on the expected, defined outcomes. Do we not want all children to develop effective language and communication skills? Do we not want all children to gain understanding and use of logic and mathematics? Do we not want these things as much as we want them to be physically healthy and to know that they are loved?

What about the child's self-esteem? The research in this area seems quite clear. It says that self-esteem or self-concept is a cognitive structure involving who you believe that you are. This structure is built within a person, not given to him or her. Children develop positive self-concepts through experiences of success throughout their lives. Children who have excellent language and mathematical skills generally perform better in school than children who do not, and they also generally have higher self-esteem.[28]

Martin Gardiner has shown in another of his studies that music training can support powerful thinking in different areas. He terms this phenomenon "mental stretching." Specifically, it is the cross-fertilization between two different areas in ways that are mutually beneficial.[29] In his study, children receiving music training experienced positive correlations between music and academic achievement, but other important changes were also found. The changes were improvements in class participation, following directions, cooperation with the teacher, cooperation with peers, improvement in self-motivation, self-esteem, responsibility, and initiative. These changes were noted by the students themselves as well as by their teachers.

Developmentally Appropriate Listening

Have you ever dropped something onto the floor near your infant or made an unexpected noise? Something as simple as a sneeze or cough can be so frightening it reduces newborns to tears. The hearing of babies and toddlers is developmental, just like every other aspect of the growth of their little bodies, and should be recognized as such. What mother in her right mind would offer filet mignon and chocolate truffles for her newborn to eat? Who would read them the tales of Stephen King before the *Tale of Peter Rabbit*? Who would take them to see *Terminator II* before *Winnie the Pooh*? Who would expose them to hot and cold before warm and chilled? And who would even think of playing the stormy (Classical) symphonies of Beethoven before the counterpoint of Bach? While newborn babies can see and process works of great detail in black and white, they cannot distinguish between pastel colors, no matter how simply they are presented. They can understand languages of any complexity, and even express that understanding, long before they can actually use the languages themselves. And while their minds can comprehend the rich complexity of contrapuntal music, they are not ready for the volume or emotionally charged frenzy of the more dynamic works of later musical eras.

Today's information explosion, brought about by the technological revolution, has changed our culture. In 2002, it is a cultural necessity that we strive for our children to become highly effective learners, capable of acquiring and using far more knowledge than in prior eras. They need complex language skills, accompanied by high-level reasoning and critical thinking capabilities. With respect to music stimuli, a complex listening base should be built to help all of these skills to blossom, as well as to foster sheer enjoyment of the arts. Music listening and training should be a permanent fixture in the curriculum of our schools, alongside reading, writing, and working with numbers. Music programs should include singing and making music, along with continued listening and analysis of complex music. The curriculum should include some songs that are fun, humorous, and designed for enjoyment, but this is only one aspect of the program. Learning to read musical notes, rhythm, pitch, tempo, and volume should be incorporated into the program. The most important component generally disregarded in today's programs is music that *sequentially grows in complexity*. This must be included to help the brain to develop appropriately, the way it was designed to develop.

The Kodály method of music training, as used in Gardiner's studies, should be incorporated. In addition, round singing should be a critical part of the beginning program. Round singing allows children to create more complex polyphony themselves as they participate in singing songs. It will surely build more neural networks than singing enjoyable melodies alone.

The Gift of Bach: The Bach & Baby Story

Never overlook something that seems to be simple.
—Carl Rogers

I spent two decades working in schools. I was a teacher for the first ten, then a dean, vice principal, assistant principal, and finally a high school principal. I earned bachelor's, master's, and doctoral degrees in education along the way. None of this was an attempt to climb career ladders or amass degrees. I was internally driven to find the solution to the huge problem with the education system that I had come to know so well: the problem of the unmotivated student. I knew from my studies that the brain, by its very nature, was born to learn. Why, then were so many teenagers so turned off to learning? Schools were supposed to be a place where teaching and learning was the primary purpose. Why did so many children dislike school?

Throughout my career, I tried everything I'd ever heard of, read about, or thought up myself to remotivate the at-risk students. It wasn't until the birth of my daughter, Leigh, in 1994 that I began to see the light. The solution to the K–12 system problems might not lie between kindergarten and high school graduation at all but between the maternity ward and the kindergarten door.

This enlightenment was occurring at the same time I was realizing that it was a good idea for babies to be listening to Bach. One morning while my husband was shaving, I said, "Wouldn't it be magnificent if every kindergartner arrived at the schoolhouse door having listened regularly to five years of Bach? I'm going to put some tapes together of Bach music specifically for young children. Bach lays neural foundations upon which brilliant brains are built. This will be my small contribution to the universal education problem." My extremely left-brained husband, who never uses adjectives, replied, "You can call them Bach & Baby." I still tell him that coming up with such a clever name had to be divine inspiration.

So again, I did what I thought any good mommy would do. I called my piano teacher from twenty years ago, who is now the dean of the School of Music at the University of Colorado at Boulder. Dan Sher mobilized his wonderful faculty and they recorded everything by Bach in their repertoire. (Bach is too difficult even for professional musicians to "work up." Ask them!) Dan and I sorted the music into the four CDs by theme. I knew as a new mom trying to get an infant to sleep while playing music that one cannot keep jumping up and down to skip the faster or more lively songs.

The CDs are sorted by titles and tempos: *Bedtime* (slow), *Bathtime* (medium), *Playtime* (fast), and *Traveltime* (everything we had left over).

Bach & Baby, Bach & Kids:
Complex and Simple

Adding quality music that is complex yet *appropriate* to a child's environment has never been simpler. Youngheart, the music division of Creative Teaching Press, a leading educational publishing company, helped me produce the Bach & Baby series of four Developmental Listening CDs and tapes designed to enhance the environment of babies and young children.[30] The four Bach & Baby titles, *Playtime*, *Bedtime*, *Bathtime*, and *Traveltime*, make it especially simple for parents to stimulate increased synapses and lay neural pathways in their children's brains throughout their normal day with the mere push of a button. This music by J. S. Bach was recorded and placed on different CDs specifically to fit into the various settings of a child's day while maintaining the complexity necessary to help give babies an enriched environment. These recordings are not like many "Classical" ones that are popping up in children's music departments everywhere. All four of the Bach & Baby titles have won Parent's Choice recognition, and proceeds from the recordings benefit the Bach Endowment Fund at the University of Colorado at Boulder to provide music scholarships for students.

The Bach & Kids series, featuring titles *Schooltime* and *Studytime,* is specifically designed for older children, approximately ages three or four to ten and up. Again, they feature the music of J. S. Bach, only this time the music is technologically enhanced, as Bach himself would probably have done had he been living in today's high-tech society. These two CDs are produced by the brilliant Canadian composer Jack Lenz, of Lenz Entertainment. Jack was raised on Bach and has devoted much of his composing and recording career to educational children's music and church music. Jack's credits include several awards from the Society of Composers, Authors and Music Publishers of Canada. He has composed music for several major motion pictures, including Disney's *Pocahontas,* and television programs, including national network news themes.

While there has been much ado about Mozart in the last few years, Bach is definitely tops for building the brains of babies and toddlers. Every newborn should have this wonderful opportunity that only parents or caregivers can bring them. Parents want and need the very best information available to provide their little ones with an enriched learning environment during that most important window of opportunity. These CDs are one attempt to provide it for them.

As a consumer warning, be wary of phrases on children's CD packaging like "inspired by the music of Bach" or "especially designed for little ears" or "performed by the toy box symphony." This is usually an indication that the music on the CD is not the actual music of the composer but a rearranged, simplified version of his works. These CDs are analogous in the music world to the black-and-white baby flash cards I discussed in an earlier chapter—unnecessarily simplified.

Notes

1. Gordon Shaw, telephone interview by author, December3, 1997.

2. *New Grove Dictionary of Music and Musicians,* ed. Stanley Sadie (London: Macmillan, 1980), 8:180.

3. Percy A.Scholes, *The Oxford Companion to Music,* 9th ed. (London: Oxford University Press, 1955), 449.

4. Heinz Gartner, *John Christian Bach: Mozart's Friend and Mentor,* trans. Reinhard G. Pauly (Portland, Ore: Amadeus Press), 196.

5. Gartner, *John Christian Bach,* 198.

6. Gartner, *John Christian Bach,* 202.

7. T. Wyzewa and G. W. A. Saint-Foix, *Mozart, sa vie musicale et son oeuvre, de l'enfance a la pleine maturité* (Paris: Perrin-Deselée de Brower, 1912), 122.

8. Louis Biancolli, *The Mozart Handbook* (New York: World Publishing, 1954), 47.

9. Gartner, *John Christian Bach*, 217.

10. Hans T. David and Arthur Mendel, eds., *The New Bach Reader* (New York: W. W. Norton, 1998), 14.

11. Robert Greenberg, *How to Listen to and Understand Great Music*, Learning Company, audiocassette.

12. *The International Cyclopedia of Music and Musicians,* ed. Oscar Thompson, 5th ed. (New York: Dodd, Mead, 1949), 817.

13. Emily Anderson, *The Letters of Mozart and His Family* (London: Macmillan, 1985), 801.

14. David and Mendel, *New Bach Reader*, 489.

15. Douglas R. Hofstadter, *Gödel, Escher, Bach: An Eternal Golden Braid* (New York: Basic Books, 1979), 9.

16. Robert Greenberg, "Bach and the High Baroque," lecture 9, Course 721, at the San Francisco Conservatory of Music, 1995. Learning Company, audiocassette.

17. *Time*, March 25, 1985.

18. Darold Treffert, *Extraordinary People* (New York: Harper & Row, 1989), 25.

19. Treffert, *Extraordinary People*, 28.

20. John Radford, *Child Prodigies and Exceptional Early Achievers* (New York: Free Press, 1990), 106.

21. David Daniel, "Key Player," *Vogue*, September 1993, 352.

22. Gordon Shaw, *Keeping Mozart in Mind* (San Diego: Academic Press, 2000), 167.

23. Don Hodges, personal communication with author, July 2001.

24. Sheila Ostrander and Lynn Schroeder with Nancy Ostrander, *Superlearning 2000* (New York: Dell, 1994), 86.

25. Thomas Verny with John Kelly, *The Secret Life of the Unborn Child* (New York: Dell, 1981), 21.

26. Verny, *Secret Life*, 22.

27. National Association for the Education of Young Children, "Principles of Child Development and Learning that Inform Developmentally Appropriate Practice," position statement adopted July 1996, www.naeyc .org/resources/position_statements/dap7.htm, accessed July 22, 2001.

28. Anita Woolfolk, *Educational Psychology* (Boston: Allyn & Bacon, 2000), 71.

29. Martin Gardiner, "Music, Learning, and Behavior: A Case for Mental Stretching," *Journal for Learning through Music* 1, no. 1 (Spring 2000): 82.

30. Developmental Listening is a trademark of Youngheart Music

Company for prerecorded cassettes and CDs that feature music selected to increase appreciation of the arts, creativity, and thinking skills in young children.

7

Implications for Education

Of all the civil rights for which the world has struggled and fought for 5,000 years, the right to learn is undoubtedly the most fundamental.
—*W. E. B. Du Bois,*
"The Freedom to Learn"

The failure to nurture and develop the potential of the brains of our children today is widespread, and the consequences seem clear. Deprived of a rich, nurturing environment filled with complexity in the earliest years of life, children are left with simpler, lower-performing brains later in life. Securing the minimal physical health and safety of our youngest citizens is not enough, nor is focusing exclusively on their social and emotional development. Cognitive development extends beyond even the intellectual performance of an adult and eventually influences health and welfare as well. A high-functioning mind thinks, questions, reflects, hypothesizes, and tailors behavior accordingly. The problems of the twenty-first century require twenty-first-century brains.

Our system today perpetuates a tremendous educational error: the notion that teaching babies and very young children is inappropriate. Pure developmentalists may cringe at the initial sound of the phrase, but babies are learning all the time, and we are teaching them whether we recognize it or not. A complete paradigm shift in our thinking about education is needed to address this reality. Perhaps the wild scenario below can help direct our focus outside traditional boundaries.

Put on your most preposterous imaginative thinking cap and consider this analogy: Imagine a country just getting started that is underpopulated. The leaders of this country realize the critical importance of propagating the citizenry and the species, and decide to take action. They set up free reproduction schools for women designed specifically to reach the goal of increasing the population of the country as fast as possible. Their mission? Education to procreate! However, since the work of the young women is important to the growing economy and young women are far more productive in the workforce than elderly women, they decide to wait until the women are older to enroll them in this reproduction school. Education becomes compulsory for women at the age of fifty; at that time they are all sent to reproduction school for twelve years. When they graduate at the age of sixty-two, their exit exam is to bear a child. This school system, the nation's leaders believe, will ensure a quick increase in population.

Sure, there is a child or two born to the women in the schools, but overall, the schools fail in their purpose. Reform after reform comes and goes in an effort to fix the reproduction schools. The curriculum is revised, requirements for teachers are increased, class sizes are reduced. Still, very few of the sixty-two-year-olds are able to bear children when they graduate. Policymakers are baffled. They blame the teachers. Teachers work harder and harder, and more and more money and resources are injected into the system, but there is no noticeable improvement. Teachers blame the students. Students blame their parents. Everyone works harder and harder, but no significant increases in childbearing are seen.

Had the country considered making its schools for fifteen-year-olds instead of fifty-year-olds, no doubt it would have enjoyed considerably more success. It's like a gold prospector who digs and digs in search of the mother lode; if he is a foot away from the vein, it doesn't matter how deep he digs. It doesn't matter how technologically advanced his equipment becomes or how much capital he spends on new and improved diggers. He won't find gold unless he considers changing his boundaries.

People do change. The species has evolved. Just ask coffin makers. They will tell you that if they made coffins the size that they made them two hundred years ago, nobody would fit in them. We have become a taller species. And we are continuing to evolve. Consider the onset of puberty. In my mother's generation, the average age of the onset of menstruation was around fifteen years of age. In my daughter's generation, it is eleven. In his *Jefferson's Children: Education and the Promise of American Culture,* Leon Botstein notes that high schools were designed for students who were just beginning the journey into adulthood between the ages of fifteen and eighteen. Today, he argues, this is obsolete. Perhaps college should begin after tenth grade instead of after the twelfth.

The faulty assumption that IQ is fixed at birth had significant influence on the education system. This notion led to tracking, profiling, stereotyping, and holding different expectations for different students. Though many schools are trying to break out of this mold of thought, it is simply too well established. The example of the old merry-go-round comes to mind. The trenches dug from years and years of racing around the same circle cannot be moved incrementally. Only by completely dismantling the merry-go-round and moving it to an entirely new location can we escape the entrenchment.

As crazy as the hypothetical reproduction schools in our new country sound, the concept is no crazier than a system organized around the assumption that a child should wait until the age of five or six to be taught anything. When the child arrives at the kindergarten door without a proper foundation laid in the brain, teachers become frustrated. Parents and communities blame teachers and schools for their failure to teach their children, year after year after year. Teachers blame parents, parents blame schools of education, and around and around the blame block we go. Since the problem appears more pronounced in schools in poor urban areas, more focus on reform is occurring there. But despite reform movement after reform movement, the results have continued to disappoint researchers. Billions of extra federal dollars are pumped into these schools in poor socioeconomic communities every year in an effort to help the students learn more and more complex material. Every effort is aimed at reigniting motivated learning in apparently unmotivated children. When these efforts fail, as they almost always do, schools and teachers find themselves in the headlines being crucified for the lack of learning going on. We are already facing severe teacher shortages not only in the United States but abroad as well. The blame and humiliation of teachers that presently permeates the media is even more detrimental and further exacerbates the teacher shortages, particularly in low socioeconomic areas.

Andrew Gopnik, Alison Meltzoff, and Patricia Kuhl refer to the baby as a scientist in a crib. In education terms, the baby is a student ready for the world to teach him. Children are born ready to learn. They come into the world, by nature, as learning machines, and their very existence is focused around learning to adapt to their new environment. Unfortunately, it must be what is happening—or more significantly what is not happening—in the child's environment between the maternity ward and high school that somehow stifles this natural drive to learn. It is stifled when neural circuits that could be formed and want to be formed are not able to be formed because of lack of stimuli, or stimuli not offered in a timely manner. Recall the grammar studies in which children who were not exposed to proper grammar between the ages of two and four were never able to grasp a natural use of correct grammar. Children should never lose their motivation for learning. And no one should assume that babies cannot or should not or do not want to learn. As far as the brain is concerned, learning complex material is the purpose of living.

A Brief History of Education

The implications of the faulty assumption that babies aren't, or can't be, or shouldn't be taught impel us to reconsider the boundaries of the education system in this and other countries. A look at the history of education in this country reveals even more faulty assumptions. What were schools created for in the first place? One reason was to rescue children from exploitation by the labor markets of the late nineteenth and early twentieth centuries. The Industrial Revolution was happening in part on the backs of ten-year-olds in sweatshops.

In his provocative work *Separating School and State,* Sheldon Richman makes the case that compulsory education was designed from its inception in Sparta to indoctrinate children and stamp out dissent. Children were taken by the state and educated to obey the state. The modern version of our public schools had their roots in Germany in the 1500s. Again, the primary purpose was to keep the children from hearing the heretics. In 1717, the first national system of schools was set up in Prussia. Children between the ages of seven and fourteen were compelled to go to the schools or parents were subject to having their children removed from their homes.

When American leaders were looking for a model for public school, they visited Prussian schools. There they found order, efficiency, and obedience. They saw large numbers of immigrant children removed from "inappropriate cultural influences" and assimilated successfully. The first public kindergarten in the United States was designed after Friedrich Froebel's kindergarten in Germany. It opened in 1873 and its purpose was to remove children in poverty-stricken areas from their poverty and bad families and subject them to the influence of the school system as early as possible.

Compelled to Learn

The Massachusetts Bay Colony had passed a compulsory literacy law in 1642, just five years before the passage of the country's first compulsory education law. By the turn of the twentieth century, almost every state had compulsory attendance laws. Another factor that drove widespread compulsory attendance was religious belief. If colonial children were taught to read, it was believed, they would not be deceived by the great deluder, Satan. Schools were set up to teach children how to read the Bible. Learning to read has continued to be viewed as a sacred tool. It has continued to be a primary reason for schooling , and children who do not learn to read by the third grade face considerable hardship throughout their school experience. The schools consider that the older children who have not learned to read are failures. The parents of the children who cannot read consider the schools failures. Regardless of where the fault lies, children who do not learn to read well, regardless of how well they speak, move, or think, make up the vast majority of school dropouts; many then become dependent on the social system. Could schools have convinced these children that they are lazy, disabled, or just can't learn?

All of this focus on reading books has continued for decades, long after the influence of print on our children has been supplanted by other media, specifically television and video. Will we someday hear claims that books are obsolete? It is interesting to note that in 1925, Thomas Edison predicted that the invention of the motion picture would revolutionize our educational system, supplanting the use of textbooks. Edison said, "In ten years [from 1925], as the principal medium of teaching, [textbooks] will be as obsolete as the horse and carriage are now. Visual education—the imparting of exact information through the motion picture camera—will be matter of course in our schools."[1] Little did Edison know the power to resist change that is so deeply embedded in the schools.

Political factors also drove compulsory attendance. The fundamental purpose of education was to equip the citizenry to participate fully in (and believe in) our democratic system of government. Large numbers of immigrants were arriving in the United States daily, many speaking different languages and with vastly different cultures. If democracy was to survive, surely some form of assimilation was needed. The burden fell to the public schools to ensure that this took place.

Through recent history, many policymakers have continued to add to the school curriculum to help solve social problems. Courses such as driver's education and health are examples. These policymakers erroneously believed that the school is the primary influence on a child's life and thus should be used to cure many social ills. Research has shown repeatedly that the community and the child's family life have far more influence on the child than the school.[2] However, over time, this myth of the influence of the school has caused society to look more and more to the education system to act as the primary societal change agent. In America, the democratic principle that all children, regardless of the home that they were born into, should have an opportunity to attend school drove our social and educational reform throughout the last century. This drive was largely successful. Schools are considered a public good and almost all children today, regardless of background, attend school.

Attending school, it was believed, was the key to achieving equality and fairness for all in our country. It assured that every child had the opportunity to achieve the American Dream. "Children have a fundamental constitutional right to receive an equal opportunity to a free and appropriate education." Every state constitution in this country has laws that have some wording similar to this. So taxes were collected and schools were built. Then when all children did not take advantage of this opportunity, we passed laws to make them attend.

The last quarter of the twentieth century revealed one critical oversight in this plan—or perhaps it was actually another faulty assumption rather than an oversight. It was that children, by simply attending school—showing up for their free and appropriate education—would automatically learn. They didn't. Compulsory school attendance, while representing an incredible social investment in American human capital, was not the complete answer.

Today, looking again to the school system to help solve society's problems, some reformers believe that the answer will be found in demanding that all students achieve in school. This will be ensured, they argue, by setting clear academic standards on a statewide and national level and testing students to be certain that all have achieved. Failure to achieve will be met with failure to move on through the system. But this may be just another faulty assumption. What evidence is there that we can force learning, even with rewards and sanctions attached? Or as some would argue, especially with rewards and sanctions attached! Today, activists such as Alfie Kohn are calling on educators to boycott the recent movement toward widespread standardized testing. His research has shown that rewarding or punishing children only discourages learning. Children are naturally curious, he argues, and it is practices such as standardized testing that cause them to lose interest.[3]

This book does not argue against setting high standards and striving to help every child achieve them. In fact, this book is an attempt to help make that happen. However, are we again looking for the silver bullet in the wrong gun? The K–12 school system cannot and will not be able to solve the most recent educational and societal reform problem—the learning problem. It can't because of another long-held faulty assumption. This is the assumption that what happens between kindergarten and high school graduation can change the brain enough, change the foundation laid in the first five years of life, to produce high-powered, motivated learning by children. History shows us that it cannot, any more than it can make sixty-two-year-old women bear multiple children, and certainly not by using the kind of instruction that takes place in many schools today.

Asking the present K–12 school system to change the organization of a child's brain wiring is like building a skyscraper then deciding to go back and add plumbing. The endeavor would be much easier and more likely to succeed if the plumbing is included in the original blueprint.

Consider This: A New Plan

All children should have the right to a free and appropriate education. The issue is when that free and appropriate education needs to begin. The failure to acknowledge that this right begins at birth has had tragic consequences, including much discrimination in our society. The failure to maximize brain development in the first three to five years of life can rarely be overcome. We deny our children the right to life, liberty, and the pursuit of happiness when we do not ensure a maximally enriched, healthy, nurturing, and loving environment for them in their earliest years of life, an environment that attends to their cognitive development along with their social, emotional, and physical development.

When children attend school, they are typically given free text-books, art materials, tables, chairs, heat, air conditioning, and shelter. They even receive free supervision by a teacher with a college degree and, typically, some type of education certification. This adult has the legal authority to act in loco parentis for the better part of each weekday with the children. Some less-advantaged children are even provided with nutritionally balanced free breakfasts and lunches through the public school system. Others receive limited health care. What a wonderful society we are to provide all of this to our children, for free. How do our children become entitled to all this and more? By reaching a magical age of five or six years old, depending on the state in which they live.

Unfortunately, decades of research have shown us that when those five- and six-year-olds arrive on the schoolhouse steps, they vary widely in preparation and readiness. Some children come to kindergarten reading. Others do not know the names of colors and are nutritionally deprived or emotionally abused. Why are some so advanced and others so underdeveloped cognitively? Is it genetic? For the most part, educators, with the possible exception of kindergarten teachers, have not questioned seriously enough the reasons for this incredible range of ability, and the learning gap isn't closing. Year after year, from National Assessment of Education Progress scores to SAT scores, this fact is clear. Instead, this consistent disparity has served as a breeding ground for varying types of prejudice.

Lyndon Johnson must have been listening to the kindergarten teachers when he pushed the Elementary and Secondary Education Act of 1965 (ESEA) through Congress, bringing an infusion of cash and federal mandates into a basically state-run system of schools. The Head Start program was born here. This was a preschool program specifically designed to improve the learning of children, unlike many day-care programs of the time, which were simply designed to ensure health and safety. Head Start also is one of the few programs using Title I funds that has shown some return on investment in the form of improved learning ability. Almost two decades of Title I research reveal that this is the only area where this federal assistance program has borne significant fruit, and the younger the children, the better the results have been.[4]

So much research was quickly amassed in the 1990s pointing to the problem of the lack of preparation for school, the government had to take notice. In 1994, with the reauthorization of ESEA, the federal government began to fund on a limited basis a new program called Early Head Start. This program was designed to serve low-income households, including households with pregnant women, infants, and/or toddlers. In January 2001, an evaluation team summarized some of the outcomes of this program. At the age of two, the Early Head Start children had significantly higher scores in language, and cognitive and socioemotional development than a control group. Their parents had much more and more accurate knowledge of infant/toddler development and behavior and used more positive parenting techniques.[5] Unfortunately, as this book goes to press, only forty-five thousand of the millions of families that qualify for this program are being served.

Where Are We Coming From?

There were times throughout our history that child care was provided for families; sometimes it was even free. But there was no expectation that the care be "educational." The roots of early child care beyond the extended family can be traced to Boston in the middle 1800s. According to Sandra Scarr and Richard Weinberg, the earliest organized child care setups "grew out of a welfare movement to care for immigrant and working class children while their impoverished mothers worked."[6] Day care for young children was established as "a social service to alleviate the child care problems of parents who had to work, and to prevent young children from wandering the streets."

Federally sponsored child care emerged temporarily as a national necessity during the Great Depression and World War II. In the first case, unemployed citizens needed work, and child care was seen as an employment opportunity. In the second case, with the nation's men off at war, women were seriously needed in the workforce. One way to increase the number of female workers was to provide care for their children, and additional child care centers were founded. When World War II ended and the men came home, most of these centers closed. Some women, however, chose to remain in the workforce. Others returned home full-time but still recognized a value in maintaining some kind of child care assistance. This probably contributed to the rise seen in partial-day preschool programs after the war.

Preschools, however, were generally different from child care facilities in several important ways. Preschools typically operated only two to four hours a day. Also, the parents of children in these programs expected that their children would be "taught" something or at least be exposed to something educational. Typically, these preschool programs were used by more affluent parents who didn't need full-day child care but saw preschool as a type of enrichment. The definition and use of the terms "preschool" and "day care" are still a bit ambiguous today. However, day care typically means full-day child care, or "babysitting," as some parents call it. Working moms without the support of extended families have little choice but to put their children in day care. Preschool is typically a two-to-four-hour-a-day enrichment program for children whose parents can afford it. Today, the vast majority of mothers with young children are in the workplace. Since most babies and young children are currently in some type of day care setting, it is incumbent upon us to address the quality issues in these settings,

Parent Perceptions

More and more affluent parents are opting for high-quality preschool programs, while working moms increasingly need the assurance and convenience of full-time care regardless of the quality of curriculum offered, if any. However, there still seems to be an unfortunate lack of concern or understanding about the ideal environments necessary for fostering the cognitive development of children across the board.

Today, poverty in early childhood is closely tied to low literacy rates and, later, the likelihood of incomplete schooling. On July 27,

2001, the White House sponsored a Summit on Early Childhood Cognitive Development. G. Reid Lyon, chief of the Child Development and Behavior Branch of the National Institutes of Health, reported estimates that every forty-four seconds, a baby in this country is born into poverty. There is evidence that we have known for almost two centuries that poverty begets poverty and lower school achievement. However, Lyon also pointed out that in 1998, a quarter of our country's children without the noted risk factors (poverty, single-family homes, uneducated parents) arrived at the kindergarten door not ready to learn.[6] Why is this?

Again, a faulty assumption may be to blame. Many people believe that more educated parents have a greater understanding of their children's cognitive development and are consequently better meeting their children's cognitive needs. A national phone survey conducted in June and July 2000 by Zero to Three, Civitas Initiative, and Brio Corporation found otherwise. Shockingly, 62 percent of parents surveyed said that children do not take in and react to the world around them until they are two months old or older. Almost a fourth of them said that this doesn't happen until the child is one year old or older. When parents were presented with a scenario that described a twelve-month-old turning TV buttons on the remote control off and on repeatedly, 39 percent said the child was behaving vengefully to get back at his or her parents. Research tells us that a child of this young age couldn't possibly be motivated by revenge and that most likely the child was exploring the cause and effect of the remote control buttons on the television set. After all, the remote control is separated from the television. It does not have to physically touch the set to affect the picture. This is illogical to a young child and is a phenomenon that certainly merits exploration.

Another sad fact was that 62 percent of parents said that educational television was "very effective" in helping two-year-olds develop intellectually. Another 48 percent said that solitary play at the computer at age two was "very effective." Sixty-one percent of these parents said it is appropriate to spank a child as a regular form of punishment. Thirty-seven percent expressed the opinion that this is also appropriate at age two and younger.[7] The widespread parental misunderstandings of their young children beg for some kind of educational intervention.

One of the popular "educationalese" phrases of recent times has been that we should provide a "seamless" education for children. The implication is that we need help with transitions for children between school levels—elementary school to middle school to high school, and on to higher education. But this concept has not been systematically applied to the years between the maternity ward and the kindergarten classroom. This oversight causes the rest of the educational fabric to unravel. The five-year-old brain is already an intricately networked organ that ineffective teachers or peer pressure cannot easily rewire. Bruce Perry, speaking to the Houston Area Association for the Education of Young Children on September 8, 2001, said, "The five-year-old brain is 90 percent formed. Once it is organized, it is extremely hard to change or reorganize it." Perry used house construction as an analogy. Once a house is built, it is hard to go back through and reconstruct electrical wiring. However, with proper planning, those complex and critical functions can be put into place without difficulty.

Knowing this, we must ask some serious questions. What educational resources or instructions are new parents given when they leave the maternity ward at the hospital with their new baby? Why is the learning land of milk and honey denied children until the magic age five or six? Why are many children given free meals when they arrive at school but are not assured of proper nutrition in the earliest years of their lives, when nutrition is so much more important for brain development? Which is more critical for development: that a high school teenager take physical education, or that a newborn's parents have up-to-date knowledge and assistance on how to foster their baby's social, emotional, and cognitive development?

The Right to Information

Most parents have high hopes for their newborn baby, regardless of race, religion, socioeconomic level, or other factors. Parents naturally aspire to success and happiness for their children. Many parents leave their home countries and risk their lives to provide these opportunities for their young children in other countries.

As discussed earlier, Hart and Risely documented the language skills of children coming from ten-million-word homes verses thirty-million-word homes. Thirty-million-word moms generally raise thirty-million-word children and ten-million-word moms generally raise ten-million-word children. What if you come to the realization that you are a ten-million-word mom or caregiver instead of a thirty-million-word mom or caregiver? What can you do to be sure your child becomes a thirty-million-word child? How do you get what you need to provide the best start in life for the cognitive development of your baby? Presently in the United States, the availability of these resources is dependent upon your socioeconomic status and the availability of services in your area. As has been the case for generation after generation, the wealthy find or buy enrichment for their babies' environments, and these children arrive at the kindergarten door considerably more ready to learn—that is, ready to learn what schools teach—than the poor.

If the ten-million-word mom does not have enough wealth or personal knowledge to provide an enriched environment for her baby, her child does not arrive at the kindergarten door ready to learn the curriculum that schools teach in the ways that they teach it. This has been clearly documented by study after study. Research also shows that only in the rarest of cases do the ten-million-word kindergartners ever become thirty-million-word high schoolers. We are caught in a spiral that can only be broken by focusing on a child's first years of life.

One problem could be the lack of access to information and goods and services for young children and the parents and caregivers of young children. All new mothers, and certainly the caregivers of infants, need free information on how to create an enriched environment for their babies. In addition, rather than simply attempting to provide for the minimal survival needs of children, society should be offering assistance to maximize the development of these young children. All children should have a right to a maximally enriched environment, and all parents and caregivers should have a right to obtain information and services that benefit their performance as critically important baby teachers. This is at least as important as teenagers having access to high schools.

Perhaps some state and/or federal secondary-school funding should be diverted to the early years. The first high schools were built in the United States in the 1820s. However, a "free and appropriate education" at this time did not include a high school diploma or even an opportunity to earn one. Until the 1890s, secondary school was restricted to the sons of doctors, lawyers, clergy, or anyone else who could afford it. The curriculum focused on preparation for university training, primarily for the three recognized professions: law, medicine, and theology. Massachusetts passed a law in 1827 that mandated that towns of four thousand or more create a high school, but not all complied. It was not until the 1900s that universal high school education in the United States became a reality.

Some policymakers today are pointing the finger at obstetricians, claiming that it is their role to "educate" new mothers. Clearly obstetricians have up-to-date training in helping mothers give birth. Many also offer information on providing for babies' safety and physical development. However, obstetricians are generally not experts in babies' cognitive development, and they are not equipped to provide the needed training and assistance for this type of education. The job is far too vast for the present system. In addition, many new mothers, particularly poor ones, do not even have access to minimal services from any kind of doctor, including a pediatrician. How can we morally justify the fact that all children do not have access to quality health care during the most critical formative years of their lives?

Perhaps every maternity ward should have a parent resource room where information and training is free to all parents or caregivers—a baby library. The adults who affect the cognitive development of children so critically, the baby teachers, could come here regularly to have their questions answered and obtain important resources. The federal government is presently busy trying to provide computers and Internet access to every schoolchild in America. Perhaps a computer and Internet connection should be the birthright of every newborn. Presently it is generally the more affluent baby teachers who have personal computers and Internet access in their homes. The poor are left without access to this reservoir of potential enrichment for their children. The brains of the rich children get richer, and the brains of the poor children get poorer-quality environments.

The Family and Medical Leave Act passed in the United States in 1993 was designed to give workers time off to nurture their newborns, to be baby teachers. The act also provided workers time to tend to sick relatives or deal with their own major illnesses. While this law guaranteed that employees would not lose their jobs, it did not provide any financial compensation for the lost time at work. An estimated 2.7 million Americans have wanted to take advantage of this act but been financially unable to do so.[8]

About half of the states in this country are presently looking at ways to remedy this situation. One suggestion has been to tap into states' disability funding. New York, New Jersey, California, Rhode Island, and Hawaii use some of this money for women on maternity leave. Two states are considering expanding the program to include fathers or other caregivers. A dozen other states are exploring the possibility of using unemployment funds to pay for leaves. Polls show general support for this type of social assistance; however, the concept of this assistance being viewed as an educational endeavor is yet to be argued.

Child's Play

Clearly a free and appropriate education should begin at birth. But what would an ideal early childhood curriculum look like? One activity that young children engage in often and quite naturally is play. Play is enjoyable for children, but it is also an important way that young children learn. The casual interaction between very young children and their environment is usually called play. Children definitely learn through enjoyable, engaging, sometimes challenging and sometimes relaxing interactions. All of these terms are used to describe play. Another important characteristic of play is choice. Children usually play with what they want to when they want to. It is the adults' responsibility to ensure that the play environment is one in which the play will result in learning or improved neural circuitry. Another critical element of play is fantasy. Through fantasy play, young children can act out the inner workings of the brain that cannot yet be acted upon in reality. Children can be cats or firefighters or anything they can imagine through fantasy play.

Children can also be taught through play. One important part of the organization of some play environments is to promote the establishment of meaning and understanding in the child's world, using themes where possible and showing connectedness at every possible opportunity. The environment may also have multiple levels. A green plastic frog and a green lily pad and a green bucket can propel a storyteller on a long explanation of ecology, colors, full, empty, and everything else an active imagination can think of. Preceding or following up this activity with a trip to a pond will add much more depth and completeness. There are many more ideas for increasing complexity in the young child's environment in chapters 8 and 9 of this book.

Lev Vygotsky's writings reveal some fascinating insights into the function of play in child development. First, while most preschool teachers agree that play is the primary activity of toddlers and is abandoned in the early elementary years, Vygotsky claims that fantasy play remains an important element of the elementary years and perhaps even longer. He believes that through play, children are capable of achieving more mature behavior than in other settings. One example is learning the concept of waiting. A young child who cannot wait for most activities within the classroom environment may exhibit much more patience in fantasy play. For example, a little girl pretending that she is a napping baby may be able to wait for her playmate mommy to cook dinner before waking her up. A little boy who is pretending to be an injured puppy may be able to wait far longer for the "veterinarian" to arrive than he can wait to play a ball game. Vygotsky points out that fantasy play helps children practice self-regulation that they cannot achieve in their real worlds.

Vygotsky further notes that play provides ways for children to separate their thoughts from actual objects or actions through developing the use of symbolic props. The stick horse is not a real horse, but it serves the imaginary purpose. In fact, even a broom or a simple stick will do. Vygotsky proposes that toys such as generic dishes, pots, and pans provide better fodder for the imagination than plastic food. The children have much wider imaginary boundaries with less-specific props. When children use objects as representations of real life, it is theorized that they are developing the foundation for later use of symbols such as numbers and letters. Any mom or preschool teacher can tell you that children can count objects long before they can recognize "2" as a symbol representing two things.

Unfortunately, in today's preschool world, adult intervention may be needed to assist with the most basic play. The influence of television and videos on the minds of children can interfere with their own creativity by replacing it with prepackaged programming. If a teacher notices that one group of children is more intent upon acting out superheroes from a television program than stories of their own invention, intervention is necessary. The teacher can use questions to suggest alternative scenarios that require the children to use their own imaginations instead of the programmed television scenes. "But where is our superhero going? I believe he must be hungry after fighting off all of those villains. What is he going to eat for dinner? What can we fix for our superhero to eat?" In any event, adult intervention is critical in helping to scaffold the learning in the brain that play can promote. Television watching does not help children build those skills and can, in fact, hinder it. Intervening in a child's play with the direct purpose of developing further knowledge or brain development in that child is clearly teaching. It is also much more effective in most cases than simply administering a "time out" or some other form of punishment. Most disciplinary actions can be transformed into teachable moments through adult intervention and explanation.

Today we know that teaching and learning take place through play and that play is an important method of preschool instruction. But there is a wide range of activity that falls into this category. Sometimes play with dolls and trucks can lead to scaffolding into more complex cognitive development; sometimes it does not. Clearly, however, based on Vygotsky's theory, we have an opportunity to guide play toward this higher level of development through planning and careful observation.

"Developmentally appropriate" teaching in the earliest years has generally included a belief that teachers should wait until a desired skill or behavior is observed in a child before providing activities to encourage that desired skill or behavior. The work of Vygotsky and the research presented in this book have shown that this is too late. Teachers should be providing children with activities just beyond what they are capable of on their own but still within what they can accomplish with assistance. Teachers should be helping children to operate at a higher level within their proximal development zones. This increased complexity will yield more-complex learning as it nurtures neural networks and wires the brain for even higher-level learning later on. In addition, we must not underestimate the ability of the infant brain. Who would ever recommend that it is developmentally appropriate to try to teach babies three or four different languages at once? What developmental program recommends that children be trilingual by the age of three? Children are clearly capable of accomplishing this. How much more could they accomplish given a complex environment, a different social setting, and genuinely developmentally appropriate expectations?

A Social Place in History

In his interesting and insightful book, *Theories of Development: Concepts and Applications,* William Crain spells out a number of social-historical theories and their implications for cognitive development. We know that Lev Vygotsky's views were influenced by Karl Marx (1818–83). Marx's writings about human nature were not extensive, but he did emphasize that one must describe human nature in a social-historical context. For example, while he saw that people were distinguished from other animals by their language, use of tools, and capacity for technological production, he pointed out that the conditions under which these activities occur have changed throughout history. For example, the working conditions of the medieval artisan differed greatly from those of a nineteenth-century factory worker. These different conditions themselves altered the societal changes.[9] Vygotsky, of course, took this to the level of the child's developing brain and argued that learning itself changes a child's learning each and every moment. (It also changes the neural activity, which Vygotsky could not have known.)

Marx saw history as a process of continual conflicts and resolutions. New ideas, forces, and methods would arise, causing conflict with the established social system. Crain gives the example of the overthrow of the feudal system by the free-enterprise system. A new kind of factory emerged, giving rise to a class of capitalists. These capitalists' desires and new opportunities to make lots of money for themselves put a strain on the existing social order. The result was genuine systemic change. In summary, changes in behavior begat changes in social structures and systems, which begat more and different changes in behavior, and so on. Social change accelerated behavioral change.

Could the new research pouring out of neuroscience labs today help spur a similarly radical systemic change in our present-day education system? Much as the invention of the printing press changed our social views of literacy, the information revolution necessitates much-higher-performing minds managing much more information than ever before. The brain can rise to the occasion, given the appropriate early childhood environment.

We know that an enriched early learning environment generally leads to a vastly more successful school life and, in turn, adult life. Most prisoners and welfare recipients were not A students throughout school. We also know that the rich enrich. Children from homes in which the mother can afford to stay home with her children, read to them, and take them to see the world and buy them every complex, enriching educational product that comes on the market are the bluebirds of kindergartens today. However, these people are a distinct minority in this country, and the gap between the abilities of rich and poor children at age six is tremendous and growing. Why should the babies of members of a society with more wealth have more right than those that are less fortunate to develop their brains and capacities fully? Today, we absolutely insist that schools be equal and that educators treat students equally. But children today do not enter schools equally equipped. Is equal equitable? Certainly not if we wait until kindergarten to begin teaching our children.

The information revolution is changing society in profound ways. It is also creating a society in which all members need a much higher level of thinking and overall mental functioning. Our culture and consequently our needs are changing, not unlike the changing needs of a capitalistic system evolving from a feudal one. To meet these changing needs, our views about babies and education must change.

On a moral level and on the basis of the philosophy of a free and appropriate education for the citizenry, parents and caregivers should have free access to anything they need to create an ideal environment for their babies' brains. This would include everything from parent and caregiver training to resources, and our democratic society has a responsibility to provide them with it. Continuing to ignore the fact that parents and early child care providers are the most important educators in our country is a tragic and embarrassing oversight. An additional concern today is the lack of quality found in most child care centers and the lack of education of our important baby teachers. According to Sharon Kagan and Nancy Cohen, the majority of our country's day care settings are presently poor to mediocre in quality and compromise children's long-term development.[10]

Babies' brains need teaching. They all need and deserve exceptional baby teachers. We can only meet the cognitive developmental needs of babies through greatly increasing the complexity of curriculum in our cribs and beyond and improving the quality of our day care centers. This includes the education levels of the baby teachers, or, as they are presently called, caregivers. A basic paradigm shift is needed to change the view of the caregiver to one of a critically important baby teacher.

We also take pride in viewing our country as compassionate. Yes, there are good as well as selfish reasons for providing a free and appropriate education. But we also take care of our elderly. We provide Social Security and Medicare to ensure some kind of care in our days of increased vulnerability. Why do we do this for the elderly and not the newborn? Could it be because the elderly vote?

Consider this: Perhaps a free and appropriate education should begin upon the discovery that a woman is pregnant. She is granted part-time or full-time leave from her job (with pay and return rights) and enters Mommy School. She learns with other mommies from diverse social and ethnic backgrounds the very best practices for giving birth to and nurturing a healthy baby. She relaxes, reads, and discusses issues with other mommies, learning how to become the best possible baby teacher. The bonding of mothers sharing the experience of childbirth and motherhood surpasses any diversity-training programs I have ever encountered in any educational system or other program. Prejudices will never have the opportunity to take root among these mothers.

After childbirth, the education continues at Baby School. A network of mothers, fathers, educators, and health care workers is already set up to ensure that every child receives nurturing and enrichment each day. The environment is filled with complex language (mommies may even learn new languages in Mommy School), complex music, and a multitude of visual, tactile, taste, and other sensory experiences created by experts and implemented by the baby teachers. After the first year, options may include regular day care or other child care settings if the mothers return to work. However, the environment continues to be rich and nurturing to the cognitive as well as overall development of the child. Children are taught to question, hypothesize, predict, discover, and reflect on their learning. After all, studies show that high-quality day care is as good as mommies in most instances, even for social and emotional development. As these diverse mommies and their children create new communities among themselves, learning abounds. A new social fabric is created by the understanding brought about through the networking of these mothers and their children.

One Model: The North Carolina Story

In the early 1990s, at the beginning of a push for standards and accountability in our nation's schools, North Carolina's then governor, Jim Hunt, took notice. The call rang out that too many children were beginning kindergarten unprepared for the kind of learning that was expected of them, and the schools were having difficulty addressing the problem. In 1993, Hunt organized a task force on early childhood issues to explore the problem. The North Carolina Smart Start program grew out of those discussions, and legislation was passed in July 1993 authorizing the program and allocating funds.

Smart Start was designed as a locally driven initiative to ensure the school readiness of all children. Readiness has been defined as all children arriving at kindergarten healthy and ready to succeed. The initiative was to be administered by the North Carolina Department of Health and Human Services. A charge went out to communities to come together and find out how best to meet the needs of their youngest children and their families. Planning boards were set up and empowered to think broadly. The boards were also given great flexibility to make whatever decisions they deemed necessary concerning the services that could be provided with the over $3 million in funds that had been allocated. They were also charged with developing ways to evaluate the long-term benefits of the initiative.

These community-based planning groups found that they couldn't identify one single problem inhibiting school readiness. Rather, they found a broadly interconnected set of issues, such as poverty, work-family strains, lack of parent education, and inadequate access to basic general services such as health care and transportation.[11]

By late 1998, all one hundred counties in the state had received some level of funding for their programs. From these local efforts, incredible partnerships have been formed among a vast array of social services. The types of partnerships include the networking of day care facilities, preschools, public schools, family support services, and health services, including dental, vision, mental health, and immunization. Programs already up and running, such as Head Start programs, special needs providers, and other nonprofits, are being coordinated with the Smart Start effort. Smart Start funds also provide for salary supplements to early childhood teachers, scholarships to continue teacher and director education, information packages for patients on maternity wards, scholarships for students to attend preschool, and assistance to literally hundreds of organizations.

The county partnerships have even partnered with each other. Under the remarkable leadership of Dean Clifford, director of the Early Childhood Partnership for Forsyth County (FECP), other county partnerships have now contracted with FECP to handle the financial and accounting services for their partnerships.

How is it all working? A Smart Start evaluation team is set up at the Frank Porter Graham Child Development Center at the University of North Carolina at Chapel Hill (SmartStart@ unc.edu). Children who have been Smart Start participants have higher school-readiness scores than any other group. Child care professionals are now significantly better educated, more experienced, and better paid than when the program began. There is also evidence of less early childhood teacher turnover. Parents from the parent-support programs have increased the time they spend reading to their children and have involved them in more stimulating intellectual development activities; their children now score on average at or above age expectancy. Participating child care facilities across the state have significantly improved in quality.

So far, the North Carolina program evaluations show greatly improved outcomes for children and families in Smart Start communities. Time will tell if the state is able to continue funding for the program and keep early childhood the priority of the program, as Hunt intended. We have to ask ourselves, shouldn't this type of program be mandated for all children in other states?

Another Model: The New Jersey Story

More than thirty years ago, a class-action suit *(Abbott v. Burke)* against the commissioner of education of New Jersey was initiated by a group of low-income parents concerned that their children were not receiving a thorough and efficient education as compared with their counterparts living in wealthier neighboring communities. In May 1998, the New Jersey Supreme Court finally rendered its decision, mandating implementation of whole school reform in elementary, middle, and secondary schools; provision of full-day kindergarten for all five-year-olds; and establishment of high-quality half-day preschool programs for all three- and four-year-old residents by the 1999–2000 school year in twenty-eight (later thirty) school districts having a large population of low-income families. The commissioner of education was charged with developing regulations to codify the reforms. Included in these regulations was the directive to school districts to use licensed community programs for early care and education in an effort to avoid duplication of services.

In order to ensure educational quality, Governor Christine Todd Whitman established a special Early Childhood Advisory Council to provide recommendations for program design. In addition, the state department of education convened a group of experts to develop program "expectations" for an early childhood program to provide opportunities for growth and development. The expectations were then identified as "standards for programs in early childhood education" following a subsequent court decision. The standards were then aligned with the Core Curriculum Content Standards in order to create a continuum of educational objectives from preschool through high school.

Driven by studies indicating that children who had experienced high-quality preschools were better prepared for academic success, the primary intention of the *Abbott* early childhood mandate was to ensure that three- and four-year-old children were "education-ready" when they entered kindergarten as part of their constitutional right to a thorough and efficient education. In order to meet the definition of a high-quality preschool, Abbott programs had to follow these rules:

- Class size must be limited to fifteen children, with a teacher and an aide.

- Teachers already employed in early childhood programs must earn a specialized P-3 certificate by 2004.

137

- New hires must be certified in early childhood education.

- Districts must provide a master teacher for every twenty classrooms to coordinate the delivery of programs and ensure consistency of delivery throughout the district.

- An appropriate curriculum tied to the kindergarten curriculum must be used.

- A family worker must be provided for every forty families to deliver social services and parenting information.

- Districts must execute a carefully planned outreach program to inform all parents of eligible children of the availability of preschool services.

- Professional development opportunities must be made available to all classroom staff.

- Health and nutritional guidance must be a component of the program.

- Transportation must be available for all families that need it.

What began as half-day, ten-month programs later evolved into full-day, full-year programs upon the completion of an assessment to determine the specialized needs of the children of each district.

The early care and education community united to monitor the execution of the *Abbott* decision. Known as the Early Care and Education Coalition (ECEC), a group of representatives from advocacy groups, early childhood associations, higher education, resource and referral agencies, funders, and others does the difficult job of providing guidance to policymakers as they steer the implementation of the Abbott mandate. Funding for the Abbott preschool program is delivered through a partnership between the departments of education and human services. The department of education funds the "education portion" of the day, or the six-hour-day–180-day year, while the department of human services funds the extended-day–extended-year portion. Funding levels are arbitrary and vary from district to district. It is challenging for community providers to meet the standards, especially regarding teacher salaries and benefits, because of a lack of funding. In addition, the issue of directors' salaries has been difficult because of varying credentials and nebulous job criteria. The adequacy of facilities remains an ongoing challenge as the state struggles to ensure that community programs have access to public funds to provide Abbott services. In the meantime, districts are eligible for funds to create and renovate early childhood program facilities in an effort to upgrade quality. Although facility standards have been created by the ECEC, they have not yet been adopted by the state.

More positively, however, the Abbott preschool programs have offered more comprehensive services to children and families within the districts. Staffs have been provided with scholarship opportunities in order to earn the required certifications. Universities have risen to the challenge and have designed a specialized credential to upgrade the qualifications of the teachers in the preschool classrooms. Legislators have become more sensitized to the needs of young children and have become advocates for appropriations to support scholarships and have developed the Commission for Early Care and Education to oversee the implementation of the Abbott decision. Various research groups are in the process of studying outcomes of the Abbott program model. As jurisdictions around the country consider the issue of universal preschool, New Jersey will be able to share and celebrate its successes in providing quality preschool services to its neediest residents.

More News from North Carolina

A longitudinal study called the Abecedarian Project was conducted by the Frank Porter Graham Child Development Center at the University of North Carolina at Chapel Hill. It began over two decades ago with 111 infants from low-income families. Of those, 57 were assigned to a high-quality child care setting and the other 54 to a nontreated group. The preschool program was for children in early infancy and continued year-round. Twenty-one years later, 104 of the people from the original group were assessed. Below are highlights of the study:

- More than twice as many children who received intervention attended college than those who did not.

- Young adults in the intervention group were two years older, on average, when their own first children were born.

- Young adults who received early educational intervention had significantly higher mental test scores from toddlerhood through age twenty-one than those who were untreated.

- Enhanced language skills in the children probably increased the effects of early intervention on cognitive skills performance.

- Reading achievement scores were consistently higher for individuals with early intervention. Enhanced cognitive skills appeared to positively affect reading achievement.

- Mathematics achievement showed a pattern similar to reading, with treated individuals earning higher scores, though the differences were moderate in contrast to the major effects on reading scores. Enhanced cognitive functioning appeared to positively affect results. (Upon contacting Joseph Sparling, who helped design the curriculum for this program, I learned that no special music component was present, although there was simple song singing and art.)

- Those with treatment were significantly more likely still to be in school at age twenty-one—40 percent of the intervention group compared to 20 percent of the control group.

- A significant difference was found in the percentage of young adults who ever attended a four-year college. About 35 percent of the young adults in the intervention group had either graduated from or were at the time of the assessment attending a four-year college or university. In contrast, only about 14 percent of the control group were in these categories.

- Employment rates were higher for the treatment group (65 percent) than for the control group (50 percent), although the difference was not statistically significant.

The Abecedarian Project differed from most other childhood projects in that it began in early infancy, whereas other programs generally have begun at age two or older, and treated children had five years of exposure to early education in a high-quality child care setting, whereas most other programs were of shorter duration. Francis Campbell, the principal investigator said, "The study clearly emphasizes the importance of providing an enriched learning environment for children from the very beginning of life. Every child deserves a good start in an environment that is safe, healthy, emotionally supportive, and cognitively stimulating."[12]

Over the history of the United States, we have witnessed two tremendous federal investments in human capital that, it could be argued, have had big payoffs for the country. Compulsory education for all children could be viewed as one. The second occurred after World War II through the National Defense Education Act of 1958 and the GI Bill. The expansive effort to rebuild colleges and universities ushered in a trend of greatly increased university attendance nationwide. We ensured that not just the sons of doctors and lawyers but also the daughters of farmers and machinists could attend institutions of higher learning. Both of these efforts cost billions of public dollars, but they have probably brought trillions more to our gross national product. A serious investment in our youngest children today could be the greatest human investment of all.

⑦

Notes

The author is indebted to Dr. Lorraine Cooke, president of the New Jersey Association for the Education of Young Children, for preparing the section in this chapter on the *Abbott* decision.

1. Neil Baldwin, *Edison: Inventing the Century* (Chicago: University of Chicago Press, 1995), 371.

2. Margaret C. Wang, Geneva D. Haertel, and Herbert J. Walbert, "Toward a Knowledge Base for School Learning," *Review of Education Research* 63, no. 3 (Fall 1993): 149–94.

3. Alfie Kohn, *Punished by Rewards* (New York: Houghton Mifflin, 1993).

4. David J. Hoff, "Chapter 1 Aid Failed to Close Learning Gap," *Education Week,* April 2, 1997, 1, 29. Available at www.edweek.org/ew/newstory.cfm?slug=27title.h16&keywords=Chapter%201%20Aid [accessed September 9, 2001].

5. Sandra Scarr and Richard Weinberg, "The Early Childhood Enterprise: Care and Education of the Young," *American Psychologist* 41 (1986): 1140–41.

6. G. Reid Lyon, summary of comments presented at the White House Summit on Early Childhood Cognitive Development, July 27, 2001, www.ed.gov/PressReleases/07-2001/07272001_lyon.html; accessed July 31, 2001.

7. J. Ronald Lally, Claire Lerner, and Erica Lurie-Hurvitz, "National Survey Reveals Gaps in the Public's and Parents' Knowledge about Childhood Development," *Young Child* 56, no. 2 (March 2001): 49–53.

8. Debra Rosenberg, "We Have to Sacrifice," *Newsweek,* August 27, 2001, 46.

9. William Crain, *Theories of Development* (Upper Saddle River, N.J.: Prentice Hall, 2000), 216.

10. Sharon L. Kagan and Nancy E. Cohen, "Not by Chance," executive summary, *The Quality 2000 Initiative* (New Haven: Yale University Press, 1997), 2.

11. For an in-depth look at the evolution of Smart Start, see www.SmartStart-NC.org [accessed August 8, 2001].

12. www.fpg.unc.edu/~abc [accessed August 9, 2001].

Curricular Considerations

*Treat children as they are, you make them worse—
treat them as they potentially could be, you make
them better.*

—Goethe

This chapter and the next offer parents and caregivers some easy, practical, and effective ways to provide their babies with increased, complex stimulation appropriate to the development of the child. The activities and suggestions are generally divided into categories by sense for the first year of life: hearing, sight, smell, touch, and taste. However, as is so often the case in real life, many of the activities overlap between categories.

In the first few days of life, your baby will find his mother and father and others who are regularly present in his environment incredibly stimulating to his senses and, thus, his mind. Everything about this outside world is new and interesting, and baby is taking it all in. The data arriving at the newly born brain's doorstep will cause neural firings to form networks by the trillions. Each body has its own special scent, which baby will learn to recognize within hours after birth. He will recognize his mother's and possibly others' voices. Talk to him using his name. You can immediately begin reciting the rhythmic rhymes you spoke to him when he could hear but not see you from the womb. Also, ask him questions. "Bobby, can you see me now? See where Mommy's voice comes from? This is Mommy's mouth. This is Bobby's mouth."

Gentle, slow, repetitive stroking of your baby's head and back area right from birth can give your baby a sense of calm. Doctors report that this soft, rhythmic stroking helps regulate the infant's breathing and even helps the intestinal functions to begin operating. (Be prepared for that first urination or bowel movement as baby lets you know that he works and shows off his new abilities. And remember, that first bowel movement will normally be black in color.)

Always be sure to be sensitive to your baby's engagement or lack thereof when interacting with him and stimulating him. Does he appear to be enjoying the activity? If not, discontinue the activity and move to one that promotes comfort and security. The brain is virtually tireless when engaged in something it perceives as meaningful, but we all need downtime, especially babies. It is not recommended that you strive for constant stimulation during every one of your baby's waking moments. He will need the opportunity to seek out interests for himself in addition to those interesting activities that you provide for him.

Expecting

When parents find out that they are going to have a child, they are commonly referred to as "expecting." Expecting what? Expecting a baby to be born. And in the vast majority of cases, it is born. Then parents expect their children to sit, stand up, walk, and talk. And again in the vast majority of cases, they do. Only children who have specific neurological or physiological problems fail to achieve these expected developmental milestones.

Much research has been conducted over the years on the role of expectations for children. In the late 1960s, Robert Rosenthal and Lenore Jacobson released results of a study they conducted involving teacher expectations.[1] They told teachers that certain students in their classrooms, selected randomly, should be expected to make above-average intellectual gains over the course of the year. The students did, in fact, make above-average gains, apparently based on nothing more than the teachers' expectations for them to. This self-fulfilling prophecy was termed the Pygmalion Effect (after the mythological king, Pygmalion, who created a statue and then "expected" it into real life). The researchers wrote a book with the same title and received tremendous media attention.

There are many different ways that expectations can be relayed between teacher and student, parent and child. Some are negative and most are quite subtle. Some involve no more than a facial expression. It is critical that parents and caregivers approach their interactions with an attitude of joy and hope as well as realistic expectations. Leave all judgment and criticism and despair outside of the nursery. If you experience a feeling of disappointment concerning the development of your child, check your motives.

Note that helping children to accomplish what they are already happily attempting is a far cry from pressuring children. Development is not a race, it is a process: the process of living. The parents and caregivers must see themselves in the role of facilitators to be good baby teachers.

Misunderstanding the Misunderstandings

Can parents and caregivers push their children too much in attempts to stimulate their brain development? The answer is absolutely and resoundingly "yes!" This is largely because of misunderstandings of exactly how to stimulate young brains and of the stress factor in forming neural connections. Parents or caregivers who try to force their young children through stages of development by pushing the children to function at inappropriate levels and with capacities that are not ready to be in use are asking for trouble. Because of the stress connection, parents who pressure babies to undertake activities before they are ready for them can actually inhibit their children's development in attaining that particular skill.

However, most of the time, this becomes obvious and we do not need a PET scan to tell us to stop a particular activity. For example, few parents try to force their four-month-olds to get up and walk. They do, however, walk around their children. They bring their children to places where they constantly see walking modeled by other humans, including other children. And parents almost intuitively know when to support their child by holding her up by her two little hands to imitate a walking position. If they were to let go, the child would fall. Few parents repeatedly try to get their children to stand over and over at the expense of bumping and bruising their babies. And most parents today are not interested in when their babies walk, just that they do eventually learn to walk. The expectation is there: "You will eventually walk." The modeling is all around them, and undue pressure is absent. "I don't care when you walk. I will help you when the time comes. I will know when the time comes by close observation of your development and providing opportunities for you to practice by cruising along a soft couch and so on." Sensitive caregiver *responsiveness* is the key.

Some parents may poke fun at parents or caregivers who actively attempt to create an enriched learning environment for their children with such materials as flash cards of letters and numbers. Sixty-eight percent of parents believe that these are "very effective" in developing their child's intellect. Symbolic understanding probably cannot be hurried, any more than walking can. However, when the time for that understanding does arrive, which baby will learn better? The one who has seen the letter "A" repeated with the accompanying sound, or the one who has never seen one? Flash cards should be used to supplement real life, not take the place of it. A cardboard picture of an apple is no replacement for looking at a real apple—feeling the apple, smelling the apple, rolling the apple, and, of course, tasting the apple. However, if after an enriching trip to the supermarket Mommy shows the baby an apple and then shows him the flash card of the apple, the child may learn the symbolic representation of the real apple and it may be meaningful to the child. Only future neurological studies will be able to tell us this on a cellular level.

Pictures of letters mean little to a child who has not developed symbolic representation. In addition, apart from their sound, letters are relatively unimportant. Parents would do much better to teach their toddlers the sounds of letters and not confuse them with the letter names. For example, by repeating that the letter "I" is pronounced "eye" over and over until the child can parrot the sound, parents may create confusion for the child when he attempts to pronounce words such as "pig" or "little." Which is more important, a child reciting the alphabet letter names, or decoding the sounds of letters to create words? Think of your toddler navigating your house. Would you force her to memorize a map before exploring the different rooms? Would you wait until she is developmentally ready to understand that a map is a symbolic representation of the house? Of course not. The same applies to letters and language. The sounds of letters and quantities represented by numbers are best taught in context. Teach sounds, words, and language by using them. The letters will come along in due time.

An important key to a baby's cognitive development is in the interaction between the baby and other people or baby teachers. If the baby and caregiver are enjoying an activity that is stress-free and happy, the baby will gain from it regardless of whether he learns to match the sound of a letter with the letter's symbol. However, if the teacher becomes frustrated with the baby's failure to "understand" what is going on, this will make a negative impression. The disappointment and disapproval will be perceived by the child and will create stress and discomfort. In these cases, the "stimulation" would be best left undone in the first place.

Attentive, observant baby teachers are more likely to detect problems earlier on, thus accelerating their chances of overcoming or correcting these problems with the least amount of damage to the child. For example, in the United States, the technology to detect hearing problems right from birth has been available for years. However, doctors initially would only use this technology if there was an obvious problem. We have learned since this time that hearing problems beget speech and language problems, and the time lost usually cannot be made up. The sooner a hearing problem is detected, the greater the chance of minimizing damage to speech and language development. Several states now mandate a hearing test before a baby leaves the maternity ward. The sad part of the story is that most states do not. Therefore we are knowingly allowing children with hearing problems to falter, unnecessarily harming their lives forever.

Too Much TV?

In 1999, the American Academy of Pediatrics released a statement recommending that no children be permitted to watch television or videos before their second birthday.[2] Why would fifty-five thousand pediatricians take such a stand? The new technologies in brain research show us why. Some activities are clearly brain builders, while others cause boredom and inactivity.

When studies showed the ease with which babies and young children could pick up a second or third language, some parents bought videos in French and Spanish and parked their infants in front of the television or computer. These children did not pick up languages this way. Clearly something was missing. Today, it is believed that the crucial missing element was that of communicative interaction.

Hearing talking and being talked with have very different effects on the brain. Communicative interaction involves talking *to* someone, receiving some kind of feedback, and constructing a response to that feedback. It is an exchange of language, verbal and nonverbal—a dialogue, if you will. By being spoken to, questioned, and looked at with anticipation and experiencing the wait time needed for a response, babies begin to pick up the rhythm and flow of language in addition to some sense of the purpose of it. They learn that one person generally speaks at a time. And they learn that they are expected to respond. The slightest little response, a smile or a coo, perhaps, elicits tremendous joy from the speaker. From the baby's brain's perspective, clearly this is an activity in which the baby wants to take part. Watching people talk to one another on television does not engage a baby's brain in this way.

Research has shown us that reading a story or hearing a story has a profoundly different impact on our brains than watching that same story played out on a screen. When a child, or even an adult, is hearing or reading a story, the imagination area of the brain—the prefrontal cortex area—is highly active. When reading, the eyes may only be looking at little black symbols on a white page, but the mind's eye is busy creating the image for the brain.

Many studies throughout the 1990s have driven home the importance of visualization and imagination. We hear repeatedly that we must visualize our goals and plan for our future to see those plans realized. This is the job of the prefrontal cortex. Gifted children spend significantly more time "hanging out" in their prefrontal cortex—imagining, playing pretend—than average children.[3] This area is strongly linked to overall intelligence. The recent study of a slice of Albert Einstein's brain showed that his neural networks helped him to imagine himself riding on a light beam. His amazing thinking landed him the title "Man of the Millennium."

Clearly one of the most important brain-stimulation activities you can engage in with your child is to read to him. On a personal note, I will add that the most important brain-stimulation activity that you can do for *yourself* is to read. I began my own personal boycott of television as entertainment over a decade ago. At the time, I was responsible for discipline at a large comprehensive high school. I was surprised how often disciplinary issues involved the use of drugs or alcohol and even more surprised at how common it was to find alcohol problems in the homes of those students as well. One night I took particular notice of the advertisements on television, the ones in which beautiful young people drink a six-pack of beer and then play flawless volleyball, or drink a six-pack and slalom water-ski. I saw the deception and brainwashing capabilities of advertising in a new light. I decided to cleanse my brain as best I could of this propaganda. I have never seen *Friends, Seinfeld, ER,* or any of the other popular or unpopular shows on television. I used all of that time for reading. It resulted in a doctoral degree, greatly increased reading speed and comprehension, and some wonderful ideas. I know that I changed my brain over time by changing that single daily activity. Start today. Turn off that TV, turn on some Bach, and pick up a book. And when considering a choice between showing your child a television program or video or reading a story to her, read. Do it for her brain as well as for your own.

The Toy Story

You do not need a lot of expensive toys to stimulate your baby or young child, just a lot of thought. Nature and your home will probably provide plenty of stimuli. The key to complexity is show-and-tell and play and interaction. Complexity is about connections. Explain what everything is, why it is the way it is, and how and why it all fits together the way it does. Then show your child, explain it all again, and when your child is physically developed enough, include her in the action. You should not assume that your baby or young child automatically understands anything. Showing and telling and interacting and playing with reality teach wonderfully! (As a precaution, never leave your baby alone with toys or other objects in which she may become entangled, that could obstruct breathing, or that could harm the child in any other way.)

One afternoon, after waiting in the carpool lines, my two-year-old son Bobby asked me, "What's that?" I told him that it was a cement truck. He asked what it was for. I told him that that's where the cement for sidewalks comes from. He didn't respond. Then I thought about my answer from his point of view. The truck had a big round ball-shaped object on the back. Sidewalks are long and flat and hard. How on earth could sidewalks come from there? I quickly added to my explanation. I reminded him of how Jell-O is liquid but then after we put it in the refrigerator for a while, its property changes. I explained to him that cement for sidewalks starts out soft and mushy and then hardens like Jell-O, only even harder. Later we sought out some wet cement and touched it. Since that time, when Bobby sees an imprint of a leaf or a hand in the cement, he always points out to me that the cement must have been wet when that happened.

Words of Warning

A word of caution concerning adhering to strict time frames in looking for specific developmental achievements in children: the schedule for what is considered "normal" is actually quite loose. Pediatricians' charts show that the average age of walking for most children is closer to fifteen months than twelve. Mothers tend to stretch the starting time for the onset of walking, mistaking the first leg motion for the first step. This is evidence of another faulty assumption; faster is not always better. All girls do not begin menstruation at age thirteen. Our hair does not go gray at the same time, or even within the same decade. Remember, life is not a race to the grave. Complexity in the crib is a quality issue, not a competition tactic.

Every child is different and develops differently. It could be argued that it is unnatural to group children of the same age together year after year. Children generally do not arrive into families in groups the same age. They typically arrive one at a time and often have an older sibling around to serve as a role model and a younger sibling to take care of. If you have referenced reliable sources and texts and still have a developmental concern, take it up privately with your pediatrician. And always remember, Albert Einstein barely spoke a word before his fourth birthday!

Every child has his own developmental timetable, which is usually a mystery to everyone else. However, being attentive to your child's growing developmental edge can help your timing for enrichment to be just right. For example, there is no harm in holding your seven-month-old up to show her what it feels like to stand with assistance before you would actually expect her to stand alone. With your judgment in check, you are simply offering something for your child to contemplate. With this in mind, you can play developmentally appropriate games with your child using, perhaps, developmentally inappropriate stimuli. For example, if you have refrigerator magnets in three colors—say, blue, red, and yellow—and you are working with your toddler on identifying colors by sorting them, the fact that the magnets happen to be letters or numbers does no harm. Your child is developing a visual familiarity with the symbols before she would be developmentally expected to identify or use symbols. This way, when the child actually does develop the ability to recognize the symbol for what it is, you will know. For example, children can count objects such as grapes long before they understand that the symbol "2" stands for the word "two." How will you know that your child has moved on to readiness for symbols or print if she has not had access to the information in an earlier stage?

The point of increasing the level of complexity of the child's environment is not to pressure or force or even speed up the developmental process. It is to keep the process from stagnating or boring the brain or stifling the brain's natural development. Remember, many children who hear three languages in their homes easily learn three languages. We have greatly underestimated the learning capacity of children.

As stated previously, if you are considering an enhancement program of any kind for your baby, it is always best to check it out with your pediatrician. However, your baby will almost always let you know whether he is enjoying an activity or if it doesn't interest him in the slightest. Watch and listen to your baby. If your baby is tired or hungry or just uncomfortable, it is not likely he will be interested in anything beyond food and cuddling. However, don't give up on an activity after one rejection. There may be other factors involved.

Notes

1. Janet Elashoff and Richard Snow, *Pygmalion Reconsidered* (Worthington, Ohio: C. A. Jones, 1971).

2. Chana Schoenberger, "Docs Know Best," *Forbes,* September 20, 1999, 190.

3. Barbara Clark, "The Gifted Brain: A Guide to Learning for Parents and Teachers" (keynote speech at the California Association for the Gifted Fall Conference, University of California at Irvine, October 30, 1999).

Creating Complex Curriculum for the Crib and Beyond

Learning, I have always felt, is as essential as breathing.

—*Linda Darling-Hammond*

In the first month of life, a baby's primary needs revolve around food, comfort, and love. They need lots of all three. A crying baby needs attention, even if it is 3 A.M., so be prepared to give it to him. Investigate what could be causing the crying (though you won't always find the culprit). Cognitive stimulation will be occurring naturally all around your baby because literally everything is new to him. So use this opportunity to make chores educational opportunities. There will be certain rituals that get established—feeding, changing diapers, getting the laundry done, and so on. With the right approach, these can be wonderful enrichment opportunities for your child. Add lots of explaining (including, of course, how much you are enjoying sharing the experience with your little one), and don't forget to play lots of complex music in the background.

For the first year, activities suggested in this book are sorted by sense, since a baby's brain is still organizing the separate areas for the senses at birth. While the hearing sense is the first to come to fruition at around twenty to thirty weeks' gestation in the womb, babies are born with a more developed network of tactile receptors. Therefore, they will respond well to hugs and loving strokes and lots of cuddling. The more they feel, the more data is sent from the skin to the brain, the more dendrites connect with axons, and the more the neural networks associated with touch develop.

Hearing: The Ears Have It

Birth to Six Months

🈂️ You cannot explain too much to your baby or use too big a vocabulary. Studies have shown repeatedly that parents and caregivers who speak lots of words to their children hear more words back sooner than parents and caregivers who do not. This effect lasts a lifetime.

🈂️ No activity is too simple to be explained to your baby. Examples: "And now Mommy is pulling your little shirt over your head. Where's baby? Where's baby? There she is! And now we put one arm through the sleeve. Where's that arm? Where is it? There it is!" And on and on.

🈂️ Include many questions and some wait time.

🈂️ For a primary focus of conversation for you and your baby, point out differences and similarities in everything. This, it can be argued, is the basis of all learning.

🈂️ Be especially responsive to your baby. When she attempts a sound, repeat it to her, encouraging her to attempt more sounds. Look at her closely when talking and listening to her.

🈂️ Make animal and insect sounds and show your baby the animal or insect that makes that sound.

▣ Play Bach music at ideal times throughout the day for your baby. This is simple if you are prepared.

▣ Set up CD or cassette players throughout your house. *(In the bathroom or kitchen or any other potentially hazardous area, be sure that electrical appliances never come near water.)*

▣ Set up CDs and cassettes in the players. For example, have Bach & Baby *Bathtime* in the bathroom player. Have *Bedtime* in the nursery. Have *Playtime* in the playroom. Have other Baroque music in the kitchen. And of course, have *Traveltime* or some other wonderful Bach recording in all cars at all times. (The Brandenburg Concertos are wonderful for travel!)

▣ Keep the volume medium to soft.

▣ Stick to Bach and other Baroque composers in the first few months, adding Mozart and other Classical composers later.

▣ Don't play music *constantly* for your baby. Do not play it all night long or during every waking hour. The sound of quiet and the sounds of nature are important for your child's development as well.

Six Months to Twelve Months

▣ As with the first six months, lots and lots of complex language spoken to your child is critical. Keep the dialogue going whenever possible!

▣ The different sounds made with kitchen utensils can be wonderful teachers. Let your baby discover the different sounds of silverware on a paper plate, on a plastic plate, on a glass plate (with your supervision, of course).

Wooden spoons on pots and pans and rubber containers make interesting musical instruments.

 Start with math concepts early. "I have two ears and you have two ears. Mommy has one nose and you have one nose. But look! How many fingers do you have? How many do I have? How many toes?"

 If you have access to a city orchestra, string quartet, or even a high school chamber music group of some kind, ask if it would be possible for you to sit in on rehearsals occasionally with your little one. Exposure to string instruments and keyboards will delight your baby while it builds neural networks. (Hold off on the symphonic bands until baby's hearing is better developed.)

 The sounds of birds singing in the morning, raindrops in the afternoon, crickets and frogs in the evenings, and all of the sounds in the natural environment are essential for a full spectrum of auditory stimulation.

Sight: Seeing is Believing

Birth to Six Months

 Show your baby everything and explain everything. Describe shapes, colors, and why you are doing what you are doing. Show how items are alike and how they differ.

 Keep observation objects within seven to nine inches of the the baby's face in the early months.

 Prop your baby up. Try and envision the world through your baby's eyes and match as closely as possible the appropriate angle of vision at which adults see the world. The ceiling is not the most visually stimulating scene for your little one.

🎬 Use a variety of crib mobiles or other objects for the baby to see when she is lying down. Change them regularly and, if possible, use them thematically—stars and moons for nighttime, sunshine and flowers before walks, and so forth.

🎬 Be sure to include objects with dark contrasts such as black and white. Ansel Adams photographs or other complex black-and-white photos or prints, preferably of nature, are ideal. Also be sure to include prints with discernable patterns in sharp, contrasting colors. The more patterns and the more complex the patterns, the better. The drawings of M. C. Escher are ideal.

🎬 Show your baby objects with movable parts, both parts that you move yourself and parts that move by battery operation. Explain the difference to your baby. Examples include manual can openers, nutcrackers, salad servers connected at the center, and scissors.

🎬 Show your baby your hands. Open and close them slowly and describe what you are doing and how they work.

🎬 As your baby grows older, share colors, contours, shapes, designs, animals, plants, insects, and everything else that you can find or create in his environment.

🎬 Include objects that make interesting sounds when crinkled, such as aluminum foil and paper. Choose a variety of similar-looking objects with different consequential effects when altered. Show your baby an apple, then take a big bite out of it and show your baby the result.

🎬 Show your baby the insides of drawers and cabinets. "These drawers look the same, but look! There are spoons inside this one and spatulas inside this one." Show her all the different sizes of spoons (measuring spoons, baby spoons, soup spoons, etc.) and explain their uses. Talk about more, less, over, under, beside, in front of.

🄈 Put your baby's favorite toy on a blanket on the floor. Show your baby how you can pull the toy toward you by pulling the blanket. Let her try it.

Six Months to Twelve Months

🄈 Take your baby everywhere, show her everything, and explain everything you show her in as much detail as you possibly can.

🄈 At intersections, explain what we do at green lights and red lights and what yellow lights are for.

🄈 Make stops at anything and everything interesting or engaging to your child, especially fountains, interesting flowers or plants, different animals, children of different ages, and other people.

🄈 Point out similarities between things such as cats, kittens, and lions, or the color of frogs and the color of the places they prefer to live. Talk to your baby about natural selection and explain that it's easier to hide when living things are the same color as their environment. (Yes, use words like "environment.")

🄈 When back at home, use a felt or flannel board (or poster board if you can draw) to review interesting things that you saw and did that day. Take every opportunity to make connections between your day and what you are showing and talking to your baby about at home.

🄈 Talk about the differences between living and nonliving things (those that breathe and grow and those that don't.

▣ As you go through the morning chores of putting dishes and laundry into cabinets and drawers and closets, let your baby watch you; explain what you are doing and why.

▣ Let your baby watch you sort the socks as the laundry comes out of the dryer. Let him watch you fold those great big t-shirts into little squares and rectangles. Later, he can help you with these chores.

▣ Begin playing peek-a-boo with your baby. This will help her develop memory skills, and babies clearly love finding out that your face is still there!

▣ Bubbles here, bubbles there, bubbles in the bathtub, bubbles in the air. Your baby will love to observe objects that don't fall back to Earth when dropped and that form when he splashes in the water.

Touch: If It Feels Good, Do It!

Birth to Six Months

▣ There is plenty of research today indicating that baby massage is a tremendously positive experience for your baby. Premature and low-birth-weight babies have shown remarkable weight gain and overall improvement of condition simply through the power of touch. Get in the habit of routinely massaging your baby gently after diaper changes, after changing clothes, after floor play, or after riding in the car. Knowing that this pleasurable experience is waiting can make your baby look forward to all of the activities that precede it. And of course, talk to your baby constantly while massaging her.

▣ Some doctors believe that there is nothing more soothing

🄰

than a warm bath for baby, even right after birth. A bath can help simulate baby's prior life in the amniotic fluid. The bath experience can continue to be one of the most stimulating activities for your child for many years to come. The bath helps your baby learn much about his own body. Sensory receptors rushing back and forth from the skin cells to the brain let your baby know where his body ends and the water begins. He learns about temperature through the feel of the cool or warm water touching his body. Add to this the sensation of soap, a soft cloth, and even water poured gently over his hands or back. Bathwater is also a wonderful visual tool for learning about the properties of liquids and solids. "If the cup has a hole in it, it can't keep the water in. If it doesn't, the water stays in! Just like it stays in the tub and doesn't go out on the floor. But look at this drain. The water goes down these little holes and doesn't stay in the tub unless we plug it up." Tell your baby to "watch where the water comes from" when you turn it on. (Never, ever leave young children alone in the bathtub or the bathroom.)

🄱 Rain, rain, don't go away. Another good teaching tool is rain. You can imitate rain in the shower, but be sure to explain the difference in where the water comes from. Your baby will be fascinated watching and then feeling rain.

🄱 Weather is a wonderful teacher of touch. Where possible and appropriate, let your baby feel the cold of snow, the heat of the sun on a flower's petals, and the tree's rough bark. (The refrigerator and freezer can help teach cold from a different perspective.)

🄱 Mealtime is an especially easy way to expose your baby to a variety of textures, not only through her mouth but also through her little fingers. Make gelatin in different colors and let your baby manipulate it on her high-chair tray as you speak descriptive words to her. Let your baby push an ice cube around on her tray (with supervision to keep it out of her mouth). And of course, play some wonderful Bach music in the background. As your baby gets older, you will be able to add more and more variety to this activity.

▨ Make a game of touching different body parts and naming them. Add songs and rhymes to the activity. "Eye-winker, tom-tinker, nose-rooter, chin-chopper." "This little piggy." "Pat-a-cake."

▨ Take your baby into your closet. Let her see and touch all of the different textures of your clothes, your shoes, your belts.

▨ When appropriate (safe and warm), consider shedding restrictive clothing or blankets that could inhibit your baby's interest in exploring how her body works. This is particularly important after around three months, when your baby becomes uncurled.

▨ When she can, let your baby turn the pages of cardboard books.

▨ Pain—recent research indicates that your baby does in fact feel it. If a medical procedure would hurt you, it would probably be painful to your baby as well. While most pediatricians today know this, few act upon it. Be advised.

Six Months to Twelve Months

▨ Your baby may be sitting up now. This development adds a whole new dimension to the sense of touch. She will begin to reach for what she sees and wants to explore further. Where safe and reasonable, accommodate her.

▨ Put on a hat. Put different hats on yourself and then your baby to help connect the visual with the feeling on the head.

(For added visual stimulation, have a mirror handy to show him how delightful it looks!)

⊞ The feet are important sense receptors. Whenever possible, leave the feet bare for exploration.

⊞ Baby bouncers are especially enjoyable for most babies during this period. They also help the baby with conceptualizing his body as a whole as well as cause and effect. Pushing the ground harder with the feet causes a higher bounce.

⊞ Put on some wonderful complex music and dance with your baby. Include music with different time signatures such as waltzes and minuets as well as marches and symphonies. (Aaron Copland's *Rodeo* is a popular favorite.)

⊞ Lift your baby up and use words like "up," "tall," "higher." Then lower her to phrases like, "Now we are short," "small," "lower," "down." Use words like "tall," then "very tall," then "extremely tall" or "very, very tall." When moving down, say, "Now we are moving lower, going down to the ground until we touch the floor." Use as many adjectives to describe the motions as you can think of. Your baby will want to learn them all!

⊞ If possible, expose your baby to other languages and, if at all possible, live people speaking those languages, not videos. If there is nobody around but English-speaking people, the Baby Einstein Company has a video called *Baby Einstein* that has seven different languages authentically spoken, accompanied by interesting visuals for your baby. Watch it with your baby and try to speak the words presented. Remember that fifty-five thousand American pediatricians united to proclaim that no child should be staring at a screen before her second birthday! It is recommended that any video be watched with your child and only once every few days at the very most.

▓ Count fingers and toes by touching them one at a time. Include songs and rhymes in this activity.

Taste of the Town and All Around

Birth to Six Months

▓ It's no secret that breast milk is tops for your newborn for as long as Mom can manage. Certainly in the first few months, taste is not a sense that should be widely explored because of health and safety precautions. Since sucking is critical for survival, just about anything that finds its way to your baby's mouth will be explored, so utmost care should be taken to monitor exactly what gets close to it! Fortunately, babies have a more sensitive sense of taste and smell than adults do, so there is some built-in protection. Your baby will turn away from unpleasant smells and turn toward anything that smells like Mom.

Six Months to Twelve Months

▓ You'll soon have no doubt about how important the sense of taste is to your young child because he will show you. How? By putting everything he can reach into his mouth, including that roly-poly out on the front porch. The mouth serves as the little scientist's own personal test tube, and anything that will fit into it could become an experiment. Beware! But try not to stifle his curiosity unless his health or safety is at risk.

▓ As your baby develops his own taste, that is, what he likes and doesn't like, try to help guide his little tastebuds toward foods that are healthy and away from sugary or less nutritious foods. Be creative. Peanut butter on a celery stick with raisins on top can become "ants on a log." A large, unmanageable banana can easily become "banana buttons" sliced in a clever formation on a plate. Apples, sliced and arranged in a bowl of peanut butter, can become a sunflower.

A Sense of Scent

Birth to Six Months

▨ Newborn babies probably have a more sophisticated sense of smell than adults do. It will be obvious when a particular scent is not appreciated by your little one. Spare nothing within the bounds of reason and safety. The puppy in the backyard, the fresh peaches at the grocery store, the newly cut grass. Expose your baby to them all and point out the smell of each as you smell the object yourself. Just watch for that curious mouth! (See the section on taste.)

Six Months to Twelve Months

▨ Help your baby connect words to describe scents as well as the objects from which they emanate. Line up a banana, an apple, and an orange. Take a bite and let your baby smell the different scents from the new spot you created. You can identify the fruits individually and as members of the fruit category. Also do this with vegetables or any other interesting-smelling food. It's a good idea to save smelling smaller items that are not edible for a later time when your child can better distinguish which objects go into the mouth and which are best explored only with the eyes and fingers.

Twelve to Twenty-four Months

▨ During these months, your child will be excited about her newly developing motor abilities. Tasks such as putting in and taking out will become especially delightful. Have special drawers in the kitchen set aside at just the right level for your young child to access. Filling them with your plastic bowls or other containers with lids will set the stage for some wonderfully challenging opportunities. "Stack the bowls from biggest to smallest. See how they fit into each other? Which tops match which bowls?" When play is over, make a game of fitting all of the dishes back into the drawer. And of course, Bach & Baby *Playtime* is the perfect background music for this brain-building activity.

▣ Continuing with the theme of in and out, take a smaller container and help your child put coins in and take them out again. This activity must be closely supervised to keep the coins in the cup and not in the mouth! You can start identifying coins by their names. Your child will probably not be able to identify the different denominations yet, but when she does reach this stage, the visual foundation will be laid.

▣ Line up an apple, an orange, and any other round fruit that you have on hand. Then line up a banana, a cucumber, and a zucchini. Now is the time to begin to point out "alike" and "different" and identify the qualities that distinguish items. How is a dog like a kitty? How is it unlike a kitty? If your child finds sorting fruits and vegetables easy, mix up different shapes of pasta or different kinds of beans and help him sort them out. Games to differentiate differences can get more and more complex as your child develops. (Empty egg cartons make great sorting containers.)

▣ Your child may begin the birthday-party circuit during these months. She will love watching you wrap gifts. Fold the bright paper slowly so that she can see the object of the activity. "What's inside? How will Jenny know what we got her for her present?" While your baby will probably not be ready for actually attaching objects with tape, she will enjoy the sticky sensation. Tear off a piece of masking tape and show her how fabric sticks to it. What about cellophane tape? Describe the differences in color and in use.

▨ Food coloring or paints can help show your child how different colors are created. Get several clear containers so that your child can see clearly that yellow added to red becomes orange, yellow added to blue becomes green, and red added to blue becomes purple. "What color do we get when we mix them all up?" The same activity will be enjoyable to your child if you use nontoxic water-soluble paints. While most refrigerators today come with automatic ice-makers, many households have old ice trays around. Find a white or clear ice tray and start on one end with the primary colors of blue, red, and yellow. Let your child be the artist and create different colors in the remaining compartments of the tray.

▨ The produce section of the grocery store could be the most enriching "school" that your child ever attends! Make the most of it on each visit. Show your child all of the different colored apples and bell peppers to help reinforce understanding of colors and categories. Explain what you are doing as you count out five oranges and put them into one bag. Then count out six carrots, and so on. When your child begins to say the numbers, have him do the counting with you. When he can pick up the produce himself, delegate as much of the sorting and counting as you can to him. Green beans make a good starting vegetable, since they are light and easy for small hands to manage. And if you have access to a garden or farm, take regular tours to find out where all of those fruits and vegetables come from. If possible, plant your own and watch your garden grow together.

Twenty-four to Thirty-six Months

▨ Grocery store trips become a treasure hunt during this stage. Tell your child that you need three of something long and yellow and that it is something that monkeys like to eat. Describe what you are thinking of and let your toddler find it for you. "Now I need something oval-shaped and yellow that tastes very sour. That's right, I need a lemon." Conjuring up these clues will be great for your own mental stimulation. For an added challenge, try to weave them all into a grocery store story through the experience. These same activities can be used when putting the groceries away at home.

▨ While it is possible that your child may be able to handle a pencil, it is unlikely that her fine motor skills will be anywhere near the required ability level to write letters and words during these months. She will, however, love to scribble, and should be allowed to—on paper, of course. And chalk on the sidewalk is even better! Post your child's artwork somewhere in the home. Refer to it as the "nice picture you drew yesterday."

▨ Toddlers develop wonderful abilities to tell stories. This should be encouraged, as it helps develop the prefrontal cortex, the imagination area. Sometimes a little creative assistance can provide the little storyteller with structure. Try adding a visual component. Three-year-olds typically can handle stickers. Take your toddler to a teacher supply store and help him pick out his favorite stickers—ones that he would like to make a story or "write a book" with. (You might encourage him to get stickers of animals or houses or people and not just pretty designs.) Listen to Bach on the drive home to help get his brain ready for activity. When you get home, get out some blank paper, the stickers, and let the story begin. Sit back, relax, and be a spellbound audience for your child. He will probably want to tell the story many times, possibly for several days. The story may take new and interesting turns over time. You can enhance this activity by connecting it to the day's activities. For example, follow a trip to the zoo with an animal-sticker story, a trip to the grocery store with fruit and vegetable stickers, and so on. The possibilities are limited only by your child's imagination.

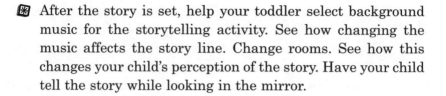

After the story is set, help your toddler select background music for the storytelling activity. See how changing the music affects the story line. Change rooms. See how this changes your child's perception of the story. Have your child tell the story while looking in the mirror.

Over time, you can compile the sticker stories into a book. You can teach the concept of chapters this way. You will see the sophistication of your toddler's storytelling abilities progress right before your eyes as he develops the imagination area of his brain, the seedbed of intelligence, and develops a sense of structure with language.

The refrigerator can be a wonderful teaching tool in the kitchen, as a child this age will love maneuvering magnets all over. Again, this can be used as a storyboard with just the right magnets. Sort magnets into categories and let your toddler select the type of story he wants to create. Is today's story about fruit? Is it about fish? Be sure to keep an eye out for interesting magnets in discount stores to keep some variety in this activity.

Have your child help you sort objects into groups. Different kinds of beans or pasta or birthday candles or rocks or shells work wonderfully. Sort them by size, shape, color— any categories you can think of. Talk about what you have the most, the least, some, a little, a lot of. These concepts will all lay a foundation for later math and reasoning skills.

Empty egg cartons can help with sorting as well as counting to twelve. Ask your child to drop one bean into each cup, then one rock into each cup, and so on. Talk about the concept of a dozen. On your next grocery trip, look for other food items that come in packages of a dozen: rolls, juice boxes, raisins, and so on.

While we are experimenting with quantities and pouring,

in and out, and full and empty, use actual measurements such as cup, pint, quart, and gallon. "How many cups does it take to fill up a pint? How many are in a quart? A gallon?" Your child will be expected to know these terms and quantities later in school. Why not give him the proper labels right from the start?

▓ When traveling, point out the red car, the blue car. "Can you find another red car? Where?" This can be done in parking lots as well. Include words like "first." "This is the first red car in this row. Where is the second? The third?"

▓ At around thirty months, you may be able to line up toys or fruit or a mixture of items, then have your toddler cover her eyes. Take away one item and ask your toddler to identify what is missing. This is fun for the child and builds memory skills. Later, this activity can be repeated with letters and numbers.

▓ There may be opportunities in your community to involve your toddler in more structured exposure to music. Kindermusic or musikgarten programs are excellent, but some may lack a cognitive development component such as Kodály teaching. However, mixing socializing with music is usually loved by all children.

Thirty-six to Forty-eight Months

▓ Some children are ready to work with printed words during these months rather than just look at them in a book that is being read to them. Get yourself some poster board and cut it into rectangles. With a wide-tip permanent marker (which you keep hidden from all!), label the objects in your child's room: bed, lamp, window, and so on. Occasionally ask your child to point to the word that says "bed." He will quickly begin to attach the symbols to the words. You may want to follow this activity up at some point in the day with flash cards with pictures and words on them. However, the flash cards alone are no substitute for the real thing. Once he has the words in his room down, add other rooms—the bathroom or playroom or even the kitchen.

- Have your child help with setting the table. "How many people are going to be eating at our table tonight? How many plates do we need? Forks? Napkins?" Plan this event out verbally before actually beginning the task of setting the table. "Where do the plates go?" Between these items, to the left or right of these items, and so on. This all helps with one-to-one correspondence, area, and location and lays a foundation for math and reasoning skills.

- Post a large monthly calendar somewhere accessible to your child. Have her help you cross off each day and count the number of days until a trip to the park, a birthday party, the weekend. Point out the days of the week and months of the year. There are plenty of songs to help reinforce these concepts, or you can make up your own.

- Each morning, discuss with your child what you plan to do that morning and on through the day. Ask your child what must be done before an activity is begun. Help her with visualizing the plan. "Do we need to brush our teeth? Get dressed? What should we put on first, our socks or our shoes? Why?" Discuss the concepts of "before" and "after."

- Come on, baby, and do the twist! If you are like many moms, you have a drawer in the kitchen full of "stuff." Some of that stuff can make for great brain-building activities for your child. Take those little twist ties, for example, the ones that come with some brands of trash bags, and see what your child can make. Start out small. How about making the sun or the moon? A flower? How about a statue of Mommy? Daddy? Baby sister? Use the statues to create a story or play. Have your child help select music for the production.

▣ To add some variety to the twist tie activity, use pipe cleaners. Encourage your child to form shapes such as triangles, circles, squares, and spirals around his fingers. He can make chains, headdresses, animals—whatever his imagination and fine motor skills can create. Pipe cleaners make great travel-activity materials and can keep children fascinated for quite a while. (Note: Sometimes pipe cleaners have sharp ends, so close supervision may be necessary with younger children.)

▣ During these months, tape becomes more than just "fastenating," it becomes something your child may be able to connect things with. Let your imagination go with your child's, considering what can be attached to what with tape. Always discuss why. "Why are you connecting all the pages of the newspaper? So Daddy can't read it?"

▣ There are plenty of good books recorded on tape or CD for children. Some come with the printed book. Snuggle up with your child and point to the words as the tape plays. If possible, have your child follow along with her fingers. She will learn that print reads from left to right and up to down in the English language.

▣ For more active times, get (or make!) some puppets. Play the books on tape and have the puppets act out the book. Your child will need to know the story somewhat to do this.

▣ Best of all, write your own story or play with your child, have your child help select music, and create an entirely original production. You may want to help direct the story toward a particular lesson you are working on with your child, such as picking up toys.

▣ Your child probably indicated measurements earlier with outstretched arms for "this big" or scrunched-together hands for "tiny." Now rulers can be a fun and more accurate means of measuring your front door, your refrigerator, or any other accessible object or area in your home or office. Make a chart and graph the widths of familiar household objects and areas. Especially enjoyable is measuring the different heights of family members in inches and then feet and inches.

Forty-eight to Sixty Months

▨ Start collections of things you and your child find on your daily outings: feathers, interesting insects—any treasures will do. Match like objects, and have boxes or baggies ready to keep things organized. Label everything clearly to help with print and word identification. Go to the library and try to identify where your leaf or feather came from. If you have Internet access, you can do this from home.

▨ To add some variety to the nature walks, occasionally have your child glue all of his newfound treasures onto a piece of poster board and label it with the date of the walk. One collage a month or one per season can make a wonderful "museum" of your yard or walking area for future years. They will make perfect artifacts for learning about seasons.

▨ Since you have been reading to your child every day of her life, she will probably begin to be comfortable with print this year, so maximize her exposure to it. Point out the name of your street on your street sign or on letters in your mailbox.

▨ Discuss the locations of neighbors' houses with words like "closer" and "farther" and count how many houses away different neighbors live.

▨ Take the poster board signs you made last year labeling the items in your child's room such as the window, lamp, and bed. Now take the cards into another bedroom and see if your child can match the right word with the item. Compose a story using the cards and words. Talk about a moral to a story, a theme of a story. You might want to record the stories in a journal for your child to look back on in later years.

■ Comfort with numbers is probably catching up with your child's understanding of quantity, so looking up your own address and phone number in the phone book or on the computer will be fun for him. Continue with height and age charts and measuring anything that needs to be measured, liquid or solid!

■ Use pennies to identify different ages, days of the month—anything numerical that you can think of. If it takes five pennies to make your age, how many nickels does it take?

■ Discuss time. What time is it? What is an hour? A minute. Talk about how numbers are used to tell time. Get a clock with hands to help teach this concept. You may want to plot out the time of the day's activities on a poster.

■ Animals are fascinating to children. Trips to the city zoo or a smaller petting zoo or a farm or even a neighbor's backyard can create wonderful opportunities for discussions with your child. See if she can categorize animals into mammals, amphibians, and so on. Which animals have fur? Which lay eggs? Do the same type of sorting activity with insects. Of course, having her own pets teaches the added enrichment of responsibility and care for animals or insects over time.

■ Outings to concerts, plays, or other cultural events are wonderful for children this age and may even have been appropriate for some time, depending on your child. There are usually plenty of free concerts or plays around if there is a high school nearby. If not, check out your local museum. If you are fortunate enough to have a children's museum in your town, think about getting involved in sponsoring some partnership programs to bring greater enrichment to your own community.

Above all, keep reading and speaking to your child. Ask him lots of questions that require more than a yes-or-no answer. Always speak in a vocabulary that you believe is just a bit above the head of your child and see if he asks what the words mean. Learn new information and skills yourself. This will help instill in your child a love of learning that will lead to a lifetime of ever increasing neural networks.

Dr. Shore's All-Time Favorites

Birth to One Year

Book: *Ansel Adams at 100*, by John Szarkowski (New York: Little, Brown, 2001).

Storybook: *Brown Bear, Brown Bear, What Do You See?* by Bill Martin, illustrated by Eric Carle (New York: Henry Holt, 1996). This board book includes large, brightly colored pictures of common animals. The text is simple and repetitive, and it rhymes. The unique feature of this book is that it engages the image area of the brain. The text on one page says, "I see a red bird looking at me." The red bird does not appear until the following page. The child hears the words and then envisions the red bird before actually seeing it. Then, while the child is seeing the red bird, the text reads, "Red bird, red bird, what do you see?" "I see a blue horse looking at me." The reader must again turn the page before the blue horse is visible.

Music: Bach & Baby *Bedtime, Bathtime, Playtime,* and *Traveltime.* This series of CDs features the music of Johann Sebastian

Bach. The CDs are thematically arranged to match the different moods or activities of the child's day and provide complex audio stimulation in a developmentally appropriate format.

Video: None. However, if absolutely necessary, *Baby Einstein* by the Baby Einstein Company. This video features visuals with sharp contrasting colors and poetry and phrases in seven different languages spoken with authentic accents.

One Year to Two Years

Books: *Go, Dog, Go* and *Hop on Pop*, by P. E. Eastman (New York: Random House, 1992).

Music: Bach & Baby *Bedtime, Bathtime, Playtime,* and *Traveltime.*

Video: Home videos of your child and family engaging in enjoyable activities can help build your child's memory. These should be watched together and narrated by you.

Two Years to Three Years

Books: *The Rainbow Fish*, by Mark Pfister (New York: North South Books, 1992); and *The Snow Child: A Russian Folktale*, by Freya Littledale (New York: Scholastic, 1989).

Music: *Teacher's Pet*, cassette by Beth Frack (www.Beth-Frack.org); and the Brandenburg Concertos by J. S. Bach.

Video: *Silly Willy Workout*, by Brenda Colgate (Freeport, N.Y.: Educational Activities Inc. 1998); phone 800-645-3739; *The Many Adventures of Winnie the Pooh*, Walt Disney Masterpiece Collection; *Baby Van Gogh* and *Baby Shakespeare* by the Baby Einstein Company. (Most of the Barney and Richard Scarry videos are educational and have excellent character-building stories as well.)

Four Years to Five Years

Books: *James Herriot's Treasury for Children* (New York: St. Martin's Press, 1992).

Music: Bach & Kids *Schooltime* and *Studytime*, by Rebecca Shore; *A.E.I.O.& U.*, cassette by Beth Frack (www.BethFrack .org).

Video: *Between the Lions* series by PBS; and *Dr. Seuss's Orchestra.*

For an excellent resource and activity guide for children ages one through twelve, see Marian Diamond and Janet Hopson's *Magic Trees of the Mind* (New York: Plume, 1999).

Conclusion

If you care for your own children, you must take an interest in all, for your children must go on living in the world made by all children.
                                                   —Eleanor Roosevelt, 1933

This book is optimistic. Many ideas are presented here in an effort to help turn the tide of unintended infant neglect into a paradigm shift for parents, caregivers, and the entire educational and social system. The present system assumes that the earth is flat. It is my belief, with respect to brain development and building lives, that the effects of a child's environment between the kindergarten years and high school graduation on their neural networks pale in comparison to the effects of the environment between birth and kindergarten. We have been focusing on the K–12 education system in this and other countries to "fix" the child who does not love learning. We have blamed teachers, programs, parents, and even other children for our schools' failures. But the solution to the K–12 system's problems lies between the maternity ward and the kindergarten door, and we need visionary educational leadership to make this paradigm shift happen.

I had the good fortune of taking an English class while attending the University of California at Berkeley that was as devoted to lifting our social consciousness as teaching us English. I recall the professor leading us along (through questioning) to addressing the dirty problem of litter in the city. With all of the homeless people in Berkeley in the 1970s, litter was literally everywhere you looked. One student finally remarked, "Well, who is responsible, then? Surely you don't expect *us* to pick up all of the litter in this city!" To this she replied, "Only if you see it."

Society doesn't fully "see" the neglect of the infant brain yet. If it did, there would be high-quality, free, universal preschool or home-assistance programs from the maternity ward to the kindergarten door. Preschool teachers would not be the least-educated, least-paid, and least-recognized educators in the system. (Actually, they aren't even considered part of "the system.") No child would go unfed—not their stomachs, not their brains. No mother or father would be left helpless until the child reached age five. And we would see the need for welfare and prisons disappear.

We can do it. This vision of a moral, just, and enlightened society can become reality. But only if you help the fire spread. The infant brain needs more attention, more nurturing, more complexity. Pass it on.

Bibliography

Abercrombie, Karen. "Wisconsin District Requires Piano Lessons for K–5 Students." *Education Week*, October 14, 1998.

Acredolo, Linda, and Susan Goodwyn. *Baby Minds*. New York: Bantam, 2000.

Anderson, Emily, ed. *The Letters of Mozart and His Family*. London: Macmillan, 1985.

Baldwin, Neil. *Edison: Inventing the Century*. Chicago: University of Chicago Press, 1995.

Berk, Laura E. *Development through the Lifespan*. Needham Heights, Mass: Allyn & Bacon, 2001.

Biancolli, Louis. *The Mozart Handbook*. New York: World Publishing, 1954.

Botstein, Leo. *Jefferson's Children*. New York: Doubleday, 1997.

Bruner, Jerome. "The Course of Cognitive Growth." *American Psychologist* 19 (1964): 1–15.

Buell, S., and P. Coleman. "Quantitative Evidence for Selective Dendritic Growth in Normal Human Aging but Not in Senile Dementia." *Brain Research* 214, no. 1 (1981): 23–41.

Caine, Renate. *Mindshifts*. New York: Zephyr, 2000.

Campbell, Don. *The Mozart Effect*. New York: Avon Books, 1997.

Caplan, Frank. *The First Twelve Months of Life*. New York: Bantam, 1973.

Childs, C. P., and P. M. Greenfield. "Informal Modes of Learning and Teaching: The Case of Zinacanteco Weaving." In *Advances in Cross-Cultural Psychology*, vol. 2, edited by N. Warren, 269–316. London: Academic Press, 1982.

Chomsky, Noam. *Language and Problems of Knowledge.* Cambridge: MIT Press, 1988.

Clark, Barbara. *Growing Up Gifted.* 6th ed. Columbus, Ohio: Merrill/Prentice Hall, 2002.

Colangelo, Nicholas, and Gary A. Davis. *Handbook of Gifted Education.* Boston: Allyn & Bacon, 1997.

Collins, James. "The Day-Care Dilemma." *Time,* February 3, 1997, 58.

Crain, William. *Theories of Development.* Upper Saddle River, N.J.: Prentice Hall, 2000.

David, Hans T., and Arthur Mendel, eds. *The New Bach Reader: A Life of Johann Sebastian Bach in Letters and Documents.* Rev. and exp. by Christopher Wolff. New York: W. W. Norton, 1998.

DeCasper, Anthony, and Melanie J. Spence. "Prenatal Maternal Speech Influences Newborn's Perception of Speech Sounds." *Infant Behavior and Development* 9 (1986): 133–50.

Dennis, Wayne, and Pergrouhi Najarian. "Infant Development under Environmental Handicap." *Psychological Monographs* 71, no. 7, whole no. 436 (1957): 1–13.

Diamond, Marian, and Janet L. Hopson. *Magic Trees of the Mind: How to Nurture Your Child's Intelligence, Creativity, and Healthy Emotions from Birth through Adolescence.* New York: Plume, 1999.

Elashoff, Janet, and Richard Snow. *Pygmalion Reconsidered.* Worthington, Ohio: C. A. Jones, 1971.

Freeman, W. J. *Societies of Brains: A Study in the Neuroscience of Love and Hate.* Hillsdale, N.Y.: Lawrence Erlbaum Associates, 1995.

Gardiner, Martin. "Music, Learning, and Behavior: A Case for Mental Stretching." *Journal for Learning through Music* 1, no. 1 (Spring 2000).

———. "Effects of Arts on Learning." *Nature* 384 (May 26, 1996): 192.

Gartner, Heinz. *John Christian Bach: Mozart's Friend and Mentor.* Translated by Reinhard G. Pauly. Portland, Ore.: Amadeus Press, 1989.

Gass, Robert, with Kathleen Brehony. *Chanting: Discovering Spirit in Sound.* New York: Broadway Books, 1999.

Goldstein, A. "Thrills in Response to Music and Other Stimuli." *Physiological Psychology* 8, no. 1 (1980): 126–29.

Gopnik, Alison, Andrew N. Meltzoff, and Patricia K. Kuhn. *The Scientist in the Crib.* New York: Morrow, 1999.

Graziano, Amy B., Gordon L. Shaw, and Eric L. Wright. "Music Training Enhances Spatial-Temporal Reasoning in Young Children: Towards

Educational Experiments." *Early Childhood Connections* (Summer 1997): 30–36.

Hart, Betty, and Todd R. Risley. *Meaningful Differences in the Everyday Experience of Young American Children.* Baltimore: Paul H. Brookes, 1995.

Hart, Leslie A. *Human Brain and Human Learning.* New York: Longman, 1983.

Harvard Dictionary of Music. Edited by Willi Apel. Cambridge: Harvard University Press, 1951.

Healy, Jane M. *Your Child's Growing Mind.* New York: Doubleday, 1994.

Hoff, David J. "Chapter 1 Aid Failed to Close Learning Gap." *Education Week,* April 2, 1997.

Hofstadter, Douglas R. *Gödel, Escher, Bach: An Eternal Golden Braid.* New York: Basic Books, 1979.

Huron, David. "Music and Mind: Foundations of Cognitive Musicology." Six lectures presented in the 1999 Ernest Bloch Lecture Series at the University of California at Berkeley, September–December 1999. Available at dactyl.som.ohio-state.edu/Music220/Bloch.lectures /Bloch.lectures.html.

The International Cyclopedia of Music and Musicians. Edited by Oscar Thompson. New York: Dodd, Mead, 1949.

Jacobs, Bob, Matthew Schall, and Arnold B. Scheibel. "A Quantitative Dendritic Analysis of Wernicke's Area in Humans. 2. Gender, Hemispheric, and Environmental Factor." *Journal of Comparative Neurology* 327 (1993): 97–111.

Kohn, Alfie. *Punished by Rewards.* New York: Houghton Mifflin, 1993.

Kotulak, Ronald. "Q&A." *Chicago Tribune,* "Perspective," March 24, 1998, 3.

Lacerda, Francisco, Claes von Hofsten, and Mikael Heimann, eds. *Emerging Cognitive Abilities in Early Infancy.* Mahwah, N.J.: Lawrence Erlbaum Associates, 2001.

Lally, J. Ronald, Claire Lerner, and Erica Lurie-Hurvitz. "National Survey Reveals Gaps in the Public's and Parents' Knowledge about Childhood Development." *Young Child* 56, no. 2 (March 2001).

Leach, Penelope. *Children First.* New York: Vintage, 1995.

———. *Your Baby and Child: From Birth to Age Five.* Rev. ed. New York: Alfred A. Knopf, 2000.

Lozanov, Georgi. "A General Theory of Suggestion in the Communications

Process and the Activation of the Total Reserves of the Learner's Personality." *Suggestopaedia-Canada* 1 (1977): 1–4.

Ludington-Hoe, Susan, with Susan K. Golant. *How to Have a Smarter Baby*. New York: Bantam, 1985.

MacLean, Paul. "A Mind of Three Minds: Educating the Triune Brain." In *Education and the Brain: The Seventy-seventh Yearbook of the National Society for the Study of Education,* part 1, edited by J. Chall and A. Mirsky. Chicago: University of Chicago Press, 1978.

Mozart, Leopold. *A Treatise on the Fundamental Principles of Violin Playing*. New York: Oxford University Press. 1959.

Myers, David. *Psychology*. New York: Worth Publishers, 1998.

New Grove Dictionary of Music and Musicians. Edited by Stanley Sadie. London: Macmillan, 1980..

Ostrander, Sheila, and Lynn Schroeder, with Nancy Ostrander. *Superlearning*. New York: Delacorte, 1979.

———. *Superlearning 2000*. New York: Dell, 1994.

Oxford Dictionary of Music. Edited by Michael Kennedy. Oxford: Oxford University Press, 1985.

Perris, Eve, Nancy Myers, and Rachel Clifton. "Long-Term Memory for a Single Infancy Experience." *Child Development* 61 (1990) 1796–1807.

Pinker, S., D. S. Lebeaux, and L. A. Frost. "Productivity and Constraints in the Acquisition of the Passive." *Cognition* 26 (1987): 195–267.

Ponter, James R. "Academic Achievement and the Need for a Comprehensive Developmental Music Curriculum." *NASSP Bulletin* (February 1999): 108–13.

Radford, John. *Child Prodigies and Exceptional Early Achievers*. New York: Free Press, 1990.

Rauscher, Frances, Gordon Shaw, and K. Ky. "Music and Spatial Task Performance." *Nature* 365 (1993): 611.

———. "Listening to Mozart Enhances Spatial-Temporal Reasoning: Towards a Neurophysiological Basis." *Neuroscience Letters* 185 (1995): 44.

Rauscher, Frances, Gordon Shaw, L. Levine, E. Wright, W. Dennis, and R. Newcomb. "Music Training Causes Long-Term Enhancement of Preschool Children's Reasoning." *Neurological Research* 19 (1997): 2.

Ravitch, Diane. *Left Back*. New York: Simon & Schuster, 2000.

Restak, Richard M. *The Infant Mind*. Garden City, N.Y.: Doubleday, 1986.

Richmond, Sheldon. *Separating School and State*. Fairfax, Va.: Future of Freedom Foundation, 1994.

Rosenberg, Debra. "We Have to Sacrifice." *Newsweek,* August 27, 2001, 46.

Scarr, Sandra, and Richard Weinberg. "The Early Childhood Enterprise: Care and Education of the Young." *American Psychologist* 41 (1986).

Schoenberger, Chana. "Docs Know Best." *Forbes,* September 20, 1999.

Scholes, Percy. *The Oxford Companion to Music.* 9th ed. London: Oxford University Press, 1955.

Shaw, Gordon. *Keeping Mozart in Mind.* San Diego: Academic Press, 2000.

Skeels, Harold, and H. B. Dye. "A Study of the Effects of Different Stimulation on Mentally Retarded Children." *Proceedings of the American Association on Mental Deficiency* 44 (1939): 114–36.

Sousa, David. *How the Brain Learns.* Thousand Oaks, Calif.: Corwin Press, 2001.

Terry, Charles Sanford. *John Christian Bach.* New York: Oxford University Press, 1967.

Teyler, T. "An Introduction to the Neurosciences." In *The Human Brain,* edited by M. Wittrock. Englewood Cliffs, N.J.: Prentice Hall, 1977.

Treffert, Darold A. *Extraordinary People.* New York: Harper & Row 1989.

Van de Carr, René, and Marc Lehrer. "Enhancing Early Speech, Parental Bonding, and Infant Physical Development Using Prenatal Intervention in Standard Obstetric Practice." *Pre- and Peri-Natal Psychology* 1, no. 1 (1986): 20–30.

Verny, Thomas, with John Kelly. *The Secret Life of the Unborn Child.* New York: Dell, 1981.

Viadero, Debra. "Music on the Mind." *Education Week*, April 8, 1998.

Vygotsky, Lev S. *Mind in Society: The Development of Higher Mental Processes.* Cambridge: Harvard University Press, 1978.

———. *Thinking and Speech.* In *Problems of General Psychology*, vol. 1 of *The Collected Works of L. S. Vygotsky*, edited by R. W. Rieber and A. S. Carton, translated by N. Minick. New York: Plenum, 1987.

Wang, Margaret C., Geneva D. Haertel, and Herbert J. Walberg. "Toward a Knowledge Base for School Learning." *Review of Education Research* 63, no. 3 (Fall 1993): 149–94.

Wertsch, J. V., and P. Tulviste. "Vygotsky and Contemporary Developmental Psychology." *Developmental Psychology* 28 (1992): 548–57.

Westman, Jack. *Licensing Parents.* New York: Plenum Press, 1994.

Woolfolk, Anita. *Educational Psychology.* Boston: Allyn & Bacon, 2001.

Wyzewa, T., and G. W. A. Saint-Foix. *Mozart, sa vie musicale et son oeuvre, de l'enfance a la pleine maturité.* Paris: Perrin-Deselée de Brower, 1912.

About the Author

Rebecca Shore enjoyed a twenty-year career in the public education system, serving as a choral music director for ten years and in a variety of administrative roles for ten years. She was a dean, vice principal, and assistant principal of high schools in Huntington Beach, California, and was principal of Los Alamitos High School in Los Alamitos, California. Her bachelor's degree in education is from Louisiana State University, and her master's in educational administration is from California State University at Northridge. She received her doctorate in administration and policy from the University of Southern California. She has been widely published on topics such as establishing effective school climate and charter

schools. She currently teaches in the School of Education at Wake Forest University and the Graduate School of Educational Leadership at the University of North Carolina at Greensboro. She also continues to teach music to children and adults from two to ninety-two and speaks at conferences throughout the country. She can be reached at www.NurseryMinds.com.